PARADOX AND DISCOVERY

JOHN WISDOM

PARADOX AND
DISCOVERY

PHILOSOPHICAL LIBRARY

New York

Printed in Great Britain by
The Alden Press (Oxford) Ltd.

Contents

Acknowledgements

I thank the University of California for permission to print 'Paradox and Discovery', which was given as the Howison lecture at Berkeley in 1957; and Miss Vida Carver and Methuen & Co., as well as Penguin Books, for permission to reprint 'Mace, Moore and Wittgenstein', which was my contribution to a symposium *C. A. Mace*. I thank also the Editors of the journals concerned for allowing me to reprint the following articles: 'Existentialism' and 'Religious Belief' from the *Cambridge Review*, 'G. E. Moore' from *Analysis* 1959, 'Ludwig Wittgenstein, 1934-37' from *Mind* 1952, and 'A Feature of Wittgenstein's Technique' from *Proceedings of the Aristotelian Society*, Suppl. Vol. 1961; and the Secretary of the British Academy for permission to reprint 'The Metamorphosis of Metaphysics' from the *Proceedings of the British Academy*, Vol. XLVII. 'The Logic of God' was written for the British Broadcasting Corporation in 1950.

I am extremely grateful to Mr. Renford Bambrough for the time he has given to correcting the proofs of this book.

Introduction

THESE essays start from a consideration of some of those occasions when people who have been trying to answer a question encounter the challenge, 'You differ in what you say but do you differ in what you think? Do you differ in what you believe is actually so? Do you differ in what you think is possible?'

These disturbing suggestions have been made not only to those trying to answer metaphysical questions such as 'Does matter exist?' and 'Is knowledge of the mind of another possible?' but also to those concerned with such questions as 'Does God exist?', 'Have men free will?', 'Can a man's intentions be different from what they seem to him to be?' and even to those who ask, 'Was there in this case negligence or was there not?'

Questions which not always but sometimes provoke these suggestions have peculiarities which have been hinted at by saying, 'Neither further observation and experience, nor yet further thought will settle them', or by saying, 'They have no answers'.

In these essays it is submitted that questions which neither further observation and experience nor yet further thought will settle may yet present real problems and even problems as to matters of fact. It is submitted that questions which 'have no answers' may yet present problems which have solutions, that questions which 'have no answers' can and, mostly, do evince some inadequacy in our apprehension of things, and that when this inadequacy is removed by thought, which while it is helped by precedent is not bound by it, we gain a new view of what is possible and sometimes of what is actual.

JOHN WISDOM

I

The Logic of God

The Modes of Thought and the Logic of God

I

I should like to say what I aim to do in these lectures and then do it. But there are difficulties about this. I have nothing to say—nothing except what everybody knows. People sometimes ask me what I do. Philosophy I say and I watch their faces very closely. 'Ah—they say—that's a very deep subject isn't it?' I don't like this at all. I don't like their tone. I don't like the change in their faces. Either they are frightfully solemn. Or they have to manage not to smile. And I don't like either. Now scientists don't have to feel like this. They tell us what we don't know until they tell us—how very fast germs in the blood breed and that this stuff will stop them, what will or at least what won't take the stain out of the carpet. Even if I were a historian it would be better. Maybe you don't want to know just how the Abbey at Bury St. Edmunds was run in the time of Abbot Samson, but at least you probably don't know and if only I did I could tell you. But as it is I haven't anything to say except what everybody knows already. And this instantly puts into my head a thought which I try not to but can't help but think namely 'Have I anything to say at all worth saying'— a question which I fear is by now in your mind even if it wasn't before I started. Fortunately this brings me to what I want to do. For I want to urge that one who has nothing to say except what everybody knows already may yet say something worth saying and I want to bring out a little how this happens. This is itself something which everybody knows so if I succeed I succeed twice over rather like one who proves that someone in this room is whispering by pointing to someone who is whispering and saying, in a whisper, 'He is whispering'. On the other hand even if I fail to demonstrate that what I claim is true it may still be true. Of course—for as everybody knows, one who says 'Someone is whispering' may be right although in attempting to support this statement he points to the wrong person. And everybody knows that a child *may* get the right answer to a sum although he has made at least one mistake in his calculations. Everybody knows this. But don't we sometimes become unduly confident that what a man says is false because his argument is invalid or his premises false? And if we do then there are occasions on which it is worth saying to us 'A man may be right in what he says although his argument is invalid and/ or his premises false'—a thing which everybody knows.

Perhaps you now hope that satisfied with these antics I will say no more. But no. I am not satisfied. For I am not content to show that it is sometimes worth saying what everybody knows—that seems to me hardly worth saying. I want if I can to bring out a little of how, when, and why it is sometimes worth saying what everybody knows. I want to bring out the several ways of doing this and also how it is connected with informing people of what they do not know—Unlike philosophers, scientists need feel no embarrassment about accepting the salaries they are paid. Motor vans hurry with the late editions. And very properly. For we want to know what won. But how does anyone ever say to another anything worth saying when he doesn't know anything the other doesn't know?

And yet of course there are those who manage this. They say 'You look *lovely* in that hat' to people who know this already. But this instance isn't a very clear one. For those to whom such things are said sometimes know not merely that what is said is so but are also very well aware of how what is said is so. Imagine something different. Imagine someone is trying on a hat. She is studying the reflection in a mirror like a judge considering a case. There's a pause and then a friend says in tones too clear, 'My dear, it's the Taj Mahal.' Instantly the look of indecision leaves the face in the mirror. All along she has felt there was about the hat something that wouldn't quite do. Now she sees what it is. And all this happens in spite of the fact that the hat could be seen perfectly clearly and completely before the words 'The Taj Mahal' were uttered. And the words were not effective because they referred to something hidden like a mouse in a cupboard, like germs in the blood, like a wolf in sheep's clothing. To one about to buy false diamonds the expert friend murmurs 'Glass', to one terrified by what he takes to be a snake the good host whispers 'Stuffed.' But that's different, that *is* to tell somebody something he doesn't know—that that snake won't bite, that cock won't fight. But to call a hat the Taj Mahal is not to inform someone that it has mice in it or will cost a fortune. It is more like saying to someone 'Snakes' of snakes in the grass but *not* concealed by the grass but still so well camouflaged that one can't see what's before one's eyes. Even this case is different from that of the hat and the woman. For in the case of the snakes the element of warning, the element of predictive warning, is still there mixed, intimately mixed, with the element of revealing what is already visible. This last element is there unmixed when someone says of a hat which is plainly and completely visible 'It's the Taj Mahal.' And there is another difference. There's nothing preposterous about calling a snake a snake, but to call a hat the Taj Mahal—well, it involves poetic licence.

At this point someone protests. In philosophy there's always someone who protests. And here he says, 'I don't know what you're making all this fuss about. In the first place a woman who says of a hat "It's the Taj Mahal" just means "It is like the Taj Mahal" or "It is in some respects like the Taj Mahal". By saying this she makes her friend feel that the hat is impossible. Well what of it? What has all this got to do with what you say is your main point, namely, that one person may show something to another without telling him anything he doesn't know? In this case nobody shows anybody anything—all that happens is that somebody is persuaded not to buy a hat. The hat you say was seen perfectly clearly from the first. Now it isn't seen any more clearly at the finish. The change is a change in feeling. It may be expressed in the words "I see now" or "It's impossible" but that is just an expression of a different attitude to the hat.

'And by the way may I ask what all this has got to do with philosophy? Here is mankind bewildered in a bewildering world. And what do you offer? Talk about talk about a hat.'

My answer is this: In the first place it isn't true that the words about the hat only influence the hearer's feelings to the hat.

They alter her apprehension of the hat just as the word 'A hare' makes what did look like a clump of earth *look* like an animal, a hare in fact; just as the word 'A cobra' may change the look of something in the corner by the bed. It is just because in these instances words change the apprehension of what is already before one that I refer to them.

Again it isn't true that the words 'It's the Taj Mahal' meant 'It is like the Taj Mahal.' This more sober phrase is an inadequate substitute. This reformulation is a failure. It's feebler than the original and yet it's still too strong. For the hat isn't like the Taj Mahal, it's much smaller and the shape is very different. And the still more sober substitute 'It is in some respects like the Taj Mahal' is still more inadequate. It's *much* too feeble. Everything is like everything in some respects— a man like a monkey, a monkey like a mongoose, a mongoose like a mouse, a mouse like a micro-organism, and a man after all is an organism too. Heaven forbid that we should say there are no contexts in which it is worth while to remark this sort of thing. But it is not what the woman in the hat shop remarked. What she said wasn't the literal truth like 'It's a cobra' said of what is, unfortunately, a cobra. But what she said revealed the truth. Speaking soberly what she said was false but then thank heaven we don't always speak soberly. Someone has said 'The best of life is but intoxication' and that goes for conversation. People sometimes speak wildly but if we tame their words what we get are words which are tame and very often words which don't do anything near what the wild ones did. If for 'It's the Taj Mahal' we put 'It is in some respects like the Taj Mahal' we get the sort of negligible stuff that so often results from trying to put poetry into prose, from submission to the muddled metaphysics which pretends that a metaphor is no more than an emotive flourish unless and until we happen to have the words and the wits to translate it into a set of similes.

'But,' says the protesting voice, 'what she said about the hat wasn't poetry.'

'All right, all right it wasn't poetry. And the bread in the upper room wasn't the body of Christ that later hung upon the Cross. Nor of course are there three incorruptibles and yet but one incorruptible, three persons yet one God. But sometimes one is less concerned with whether what one says is true, literally true, than one is to press past illusion to the apprehension of reality, its unity and its diversity.'

'Well let that pass,' says the sober voice, 'since it agitates you so much, let it pass. It all seems rather vague to me and I don't know what you mean about the judge and his judgements. Could anything be further from poetry, more sober? However let is pass, let it pass and come to my second point. What has this conversation about a hat got to do with philosophy, this rather bizarre conversation about a hat?'

My answer is this: Is conversation about the nature and reality of goodness and beauty philosophical, metaphysical conversation? Is conversation about the reality and ultimate nature of the soul philosophical, metaphysical conversation? Is conversation about the reality and ultimate nature of matter philosophical, metaphysical conversation? Is conversation about the reality and ultimate nature of philosophical, metaphysical discussion philosophical, metaphysical conversation? It is. Well, the conversation about the hat throws light on all that—and more immediately conversation about conversation about the hat is a bit of metaphysics and bears on other bits. It *is* a member of the family of metaphysical conversations and its character throws a light on the other members of that family; and the conversation about the hat itself is a member of the family of *Attempts to come at the truth* and its character throws light on the character of the other members of that vast family. The character of any one human being throws light on the characters of all the rest and they on it. For what is the character of a woman, of a man, of anything at all but the way she, he, it is like and unlike men, monkeys, microbes, the dust, the angels high in heaven, God on his throne —all that is and all that might have been.

'Hold on, hold on,' says the voice. 'This sounds rather like church. It's so obscure.'

This makes me want to mutter 'Thank heaven for the church.' It is often obscurantist. But sometimes in those lecture halls we endeavour to substitute for it the light seems a thought too bright and on the brilliant plains of intellectual orthodoxy we half remember something lost in Lyonesse or something that was never found. Still—I must answer that voice of protest, that voice which somehow in spite of its anticlerical bias is

also the voice of honesty, order, law, conscience saying 'Let's
get this clear. How can consideration of a conversation about
a hat make metaphysics more manageable? Even if the conversation about the hat does a little illuminate the hat, isn't
it a far cry to philosophy which professes to illuminate reality?'

II

At the end of the last discussion I was left facing the question:
Why all this about a hat and the Taj Mahal? If you want to
bring out the fact that we sometimes use words neither to give
information as when we say 'That will be fifteen guineas'
nor to express and evoke feeling as when we exclaim '*Fifteen*
guineas!' but to give a greater apprehension of what is already
before us then why don't you choose a better example? For
instance why not take the case of an accountant who has before
him the assets and liabilities of a firm and asks 'Are they
solvent?' or a statistician who has before him the records of
births and deaths for the last 50 years and asks 'Has the average man today a greater expectation of life than he had 20
years ago?' Here are questions which can be settled on the
basis of facts already ascertained and which are yet definite
questions which can be settled by an agreed, definite, mathematical, deductive procedure. Why choose as an example
a statement so preposterous and loosely worded that the question
'Is it true?' is hardly a question at all ... It not only cannot
be answered by collecting new data by observation but also
cannot be answered by any definite deductive procedure.

My answer is: That is why I chose it. We all know and,
what is more, we all recognize that there are questions which
though they don't call for further investigation but only for
reflection are yet perfectly respectable because the reflection
they call for may be carried out in a definite demonstrative
procedure which gives results Yes or No. My point is that
this isn't the only sort of reflection and that the other sorts
are not poor relations. Maybe they tend to have deplorable
associates but they themselves we cannot afford to ignore. For
they too take us toward a better apprehension of reality and
also help us to understand better the character of all reflection
including the more normal members of the family.

We do not deny that vague and queer things are said and that people make some show of considering them. We do not say that drama, novels, poetry, never show us anything of the truth. But we are apt to half-feel that what is said in poetry is always more a matter of fancy than of fact, that it is not within the scope of reason. I am urging that there is more of poetry in science and more of science in poetry than our philosophy permits us readily to grasp. 'There is within the flame of love a sort of wick or snuff that doth abate it' is not so far from 'There is within the central rail on the Inner Circle a sort of current that, etc.' 'There is between a rising tide and the rising moon a sort of bond that, etc.'. Newton with his doctrine of gravitation gave us a so much greater apprehension of nature not so much because he told us what we would or would not see, like Pasteur or one who predicts what will be first past the post, but because he enabled us to see anew a thousand familiar incidents. To hint that when we are concerned with questions which are still unanswered even when we have left no stone unturned, no skid mark unmeasured, then thinking is no use, is to forget that when the facts are agreed upon we still must hear argument before we give judgement. To hint that, when argument cannot show that in the usual usage of language the correct answer is Yes or No it shows us nothing, is to forget that such argument is in such a case just as necessary and just as valuable for an apprehension of the case before us as it is in those cases when it happens that we can express that greater apprehension in a word—Guilty, Not Guilty, Mad, Not Mad, Negligent, Not Negligent, Cruel, Not Cruel. To hint that whenever, in our efforts to portray nature, we break the bonds of linguistic convention and say what is preposterous then counsel must throw up the case because we are no longer at the bar of reason—to say this is to denigrate the very modes of thought that we need most when most we need to think.

And yet, in one's efforts to think clearly it is easy to speak as if it were a waste of time to try to answer a question which hasn't an answer Yes or No, Right or Wrong, True or False. And when lately some people had the courage to say, 'A statement hasn't really a meaning unless it can be settled either by observation or by the sort of definite procedure by which questions of mathematics or logic are settled, otherwise it isn't a real, meaningful, worthwhile question but verbal, emotive, or nonsensical' then we welcomed this bold pronouncement because it seemed to say what we had long felt but not had the courage to say.

It is easy to see that this principle as it stands won't do. Consider the question 'Here are the records for births and deaths for the last fifty years. Does the average man live longer today than he did twenty years ago?' This is not itself a hypothetical, mathematical question. It is not the question '*If* the figures were as follows what *would* the answer be?' It is the question 'These being the figures what *is* the answer?' This is a question about what has actually happened.

However it is settled by a definite deductive procedure. So such a case leaves it open to us to reformulate our tempting principle as follows: A question is a real, meaningful question only if either it can be answered by observation or it can be answered by demonstration from premises which are either self-evident or obtained by describing what we have observed.

This unspoken formula frames I submit a prevalent, though often unspoken, habit of thought. We know the man who when we are vigorously discussing some point interposes with 'Look— we must define our terms, mustn't we?' He has been educated; he has been taught. His intentions are of the best. He is an ally against fluffy and futile talk. And yet so often by the time he has finished it seems somehow as if the questions he has answered aren't the ones we were interested in and worse still we seem to be unable to say what we were interested in. For example, suppose a man says to his wife, 'The children ought to clean their shoes before going to school'. 'Oh, don't be so fussy', she says. 'I am not being fussy,' he says, 'I'm merely concerned that the children should learn the ordinary politeness of taking some care of their appearance and not arrive at school in a slovenly state.' '*Slovenly*,' she says but at this point the good friend intervenes. He addresses himself to the wife. 'Look,' he says with his pleasant smile, 'we must define our terms, mustn't we? One can't begin to answer a question until one has defined one's terms.' 'In that case one can't begin,' she says, 'for when one defines a word one puts another in its place.' 'Yes,' he says, 'but you know I don't mean that we ought to define *every* word we use. I mean we need to define the *vague* ones'. 'By equally vague ones I suppose,' she says. 'No, no,' he says, 'by more precise ones.' 'But,' she says, 'if what you put in place of the vague is something not vague then the new words can't have the same meaning as the old ones had.' 'I see what you mean,' he says, 'but still, what is the use of arguing about a question which hasn't a definite answer? One must know what one means.' 'Certainly one must know or come to know what one means,' she says, 'but that doesn't mean that there is no use in arguing about questions which haven't definite answers. They are just the ones which are most interesting—those and the ones which can't mean what they seem to mean, because they are so preposterous. For instance I said just now that Jack was fussy. We both knew what I meant —I meant like an old hen. I daresay there is something to be said for saying he is not fussy. But if so I want to have it said and I want to have my say too. Now you say that we can't discuss this question until we have defined our terms. I suppose you mean the terms "fussy" or "slovenly." But we were discussing it until you interposed. 'Well,' he says, 'I interposed because it seemed to me that you were discussing a question which couldn't be answered. You said Jack was fussy, he said he wasn't. But this wasn't a real dispute, it was a question of words'.

She: It *wasn't* a question of words, it was a real question, a very real question.

He: Well of course it was a question you and he had strong feelings about. Or rather the word 'fussy' is an *emotive* word because it expresses our feelings and when you said that Jack was fussy because he said the children ought to clean their shoes before going to school, you expressed how you felt about their doing this and about Jack—and when he said he was not fussy he expressed his feelings about this and about you. But there wasn't any real question between you.

She: What d'you mean, no *real* question?

He: Well, I mean 'Is Jack fussy?' isn't a question like 'Has Jack diphtheria?' which can be settled by taking a swab from his throat. Nor is it like 'Has he the money for the tickets? They cost 15/- and he has 10/-, one shilling, three sixpences and half a crown. Now is that 15/-?' There is a procedure for settling such a question.

She: You are not now saying that we can't answer a question unless we can define our terms. But what are you saying? Is it that questions which can't be settled by observation nor by deduction aren't really questions? But what do you mean 'aren't really questions'? Do you mean that there is no definite procedure for answering them? But what d'you call a definite procedure? Is legal procedure when cases are quoted in order to show for example that in the case before the court there was negligence or that there was not—is this a definite procedure? And does it always lead to an answer? Whenever I get a glimpse of what you mean it seems preposterous and it only doesn't seem preposterous when I don't know what you mean. But I want to *come* to know what you mean. I want to know what's at the back of your saying that questions which seem to be real questions aren't really; I want to know what makes you say it, what reasons you have, whether you are right or wrong or neither. Or is this not a real question because it hasn't a definite answer so that it is futile to discuss it?

'Well,' he says, 'I think you know what I mean. I mean that there are lots of questions which seem as if they could be answered by observation or deduction when they can't be really because they are matters of words or matters of feeling.'

She: We all know that this sometimes happens. For instance one person might say that a certain food is in short supply and another that it is not because the one means that people can't get as much of it as they want to buy and the other means that there is no less of this food on the market than usual. Or to take a more trivial but simpler instance: I remember I once said of two horses which had the same father that they were half-brothers and someone else said that they were not and it turned out that this was because he didn't call *horses* half-brothers unless they had the same *mother*.

He: I don't mean just trivial instances like that. I mean that there are questions which seem important to us and seem to call for much thought because they seem difficult to answer when really they are difficult to answer only because there is no way of answering them, so that they have no answers. For instance take an old question which has very much concerned people—the question 'Did someone make the world?' 'Is there Someone behind it all?' This seems as if it could be answered like 'Who made this watch?' 'Who laid out this garden?' 'Is there a master mind behind all these seemingly disconnected crimes?' But it can't be answered in that way. It couldn't be. What I mean is this: when you are told that there is someone, God, who brings the young lions their prey and feeds the cattle upon a thousand hills, it is natural to think that if you watch, perhaps in the hush at dawn or at sunset, you will see something to confirm this statement. You watch. What d'you see? Antelopes feeding perhaps, or zebras come down to drink. A lion springs—with wonderful acceleration it is true—but still his own acceleration. And if anything saves that zebra it's the way he comes round on his hocks and gets going. There are the stars and the flowers and the animals. But there's no one to be seen. And no one to be heard. There's the wind and there's the thunder but if you call there's no answer except the echo of your own voice. It is natural to infer that those who told us that there is someone who looks after it all are wrong. But that is a mistake we are told. No such inference is legitimate they say, because God is invisible.

She: God is a spirit and cannot be seen nor heard. But the evidences of his existence lie in the order and arrangement of nature.

He: Ah. That is what is so often said. But it suggests that in nature there are evidences of God as there are in a watch the evidences of a maker, in a cathedral, the evidences of an architect, in a garden, the evidences of a gardener. And this is to suggest that God *could* be seen. It then turns out that this is a mistake. A gardener may be elusive, an architect retiring, a watch-maker hard to find, but we know what it would be to see them and so confirm the guesses that it is they who are responsible for what we see before us. Now what would it be like to see God? Suppose some seer were to see, imagine we all saw, move upwards from the ocean to the sky some prodigious figure which declared in dreadful tones the moral law or prophesied most truly—our fate. Would this be to see God?

Wouldn't it just be a phenomenon which later we were able to explain or not able to explain but in neither case the proof of a living God. The logic of God if there is such a logic isn't like that.

She: Indeed, indeed. The way to knowledge of God is not

as simple as we might confusedly hope. An evil and adulterous generation seeketh after a sign and there shall no sign be given it save the sign of the prophet Jonah. And that is not an arbitrary decree but one by which God Himself is bound. What you call 'the logic of God' couldn't be simpler than it is without His being less than He is, for the simpler the possible proofs that something is so the simpler it is for it to be so.

He: What d'you mean?

She: Well, if we mean by 'a rainbow' only a certain appearance in the sky then it is easy to know at a glance whether today there is a rainbow or not. But in that case a rainbow is only an appearance in the sky. The moment it is more, that moment it's harder to know. If one who says 'There's a rainbow' means not merely that there is a certain appearance in the sky but that that appearance is linked with water and the sun, then the appearance is no longer by itself a proof that what he says is so. It may be a sign but it is not one from which he can read off the answer to the question 'Is there a rainbow?' as he could when by 'a rainbow' was meant no more than a certain appearance in the sky. When a rainbow is more than the appearance of a rainbow then that appearance is not a sign which makes it beside the point to look for the rest of what makes a rainbow a rainbow. The simplest people are sometimes very good at telling whether a storm is coming but the full proof, the full confirmation of what they reckon is so, cannot be less complex than all that makes a storm. Horses are quick to know whether one is angry, babies to know whether one loves them, but the full proof of what they feel is so cannot be less complex than is anger or love itself—as you say it is not merely that there *is* not some fool-proof proof of God. There *couldn't* be. But that doesn't mean that there are no evidences of God's existence; it doesn't mean that there are no proofs of his existence; nor that these are not to be found in experience; not even that they are not to be found in what we see and hear. One cannot see power but it's from what we see that we know that power is present when we watch the tube-train mysteriously move towards the Marble Arch, and the more we watch, the more explicable the mystery becomes, the more, without limit, the proof approaches a demonstration. Each day a thousand incidents confirm the doctrine that energy is indestructible:

and if the present proof is not a demonstration that is not because the conclusion calls for reasons of a kind we never get. It is because the doctrine is infinite in its implications so that beyond any conceivable evidence at any time there is still evidence beyond that time—evidence for or evidence against—until no wheels are turning and time stops. In the same way, as the scroll of nature unrolls the proof of an eternal God prevails —or fails—until on the day of judgement doctrine, like theory, must become a verdict and all be lost or won.

III

He: I understand that you are now saying that the order and arrangement of nature proves the existence of God, not as the moving machinery of a mill indicates the flow of water beneath it, but as the behaviour of an electrical machine proves the presence of electricity because electricity just is such behaviour. The average man is invisible but we may know whether he is orderly or disorderly because his existence and nature are deducible from that of individual men. He is orderly if they are orderly because his being orderly just is their being orderly. But now if the existence of God is deducible from the fact that nature is orderly then one who says that God exists merely puts in theological words what others express in the words, 'In nature nothing is inexplicable, there is always a reason why.' And those who speak of God would not allow that this is all they mean. This is why I say that the question, 'Does God exist?' cannot be answered by observation and also cannot be answered by deduction. And this is why I say that though it seems to be a question it is not. The statement 'God's in his heaven' may express a feeling but it is not something that could be true or false, because nothing would make it false and therefore nothing would make it true.

She: You make too little of a move in thought which from a mass of data extracts and assembles what builds up into the proof of something which, though it doesn't go beyond the data, gives us an apprehension of reality which before we lacked. The move from the myriad transactions of the market to the conclusion that sterling is stronger isn't negligible. The move from the bewildering and apparently disorderly flux of nature to the doctrine that all that happens happens in order is one which called for our best efforts and gave us a very different apprehension of nature. Perhaps it took Spinoza a long way towards God.

Still it *is* very true that those who speak of God don't mean merely that nature is orderly. Nature would be orderly if it were nothing but an enormous clock slowly but inevitably running down. But then I am not saying that if there is order in Nature that proves that God exists. The fact that a machine is electrical is not deducible from the fact that its behaviour is orderly. If there were no order in its behaviour it couldn't be electrical but there could be order in its behaviour without its being electrical. It might run by falling weights. It is the fact that the order in its behaviour is of a certain character which makes the machine electrical. It doesn't need winding but from time to time it stops or goes more slowly just when the fire goes out—that's what makes it electrical. The mere fact that Nature is orderly would never prove that Energy is indestructible. What makes this true is the fact that the order in nature is of a certain character. It might have been of a different character but, as it is, each day confirms the doctrine of the conservation of energy.

The order of nature might have been of a character which would make it fair to say, 'It is all in the hands of someone who made it and then fell asleep' or, 'It's all in the hands of someone who arranges the little ironies of fate.' For all I have said to the contrary it may be of this character. For I am not trying to prove that God does exist but only to prove that it is wrong to say that there could be no proof that he does or that he does not.

He: But surely this comparison of the logic of God with the logic of Energy isn't a legitimate comparison.

She: I don't know whether it's legitimate or not. I am making it.

He: Yes but—well, it's like this: I understand you when you say that just as those who speak of the existence and properties of Energy don't deduce all they say from the fact that the procession of events in nature is orderly but from the particular character of that procession of events, so those who speak of God don't deduce his existence and properties merely from the fact that the procession of events is orderly but from the particular character of that procession. But surely the question 'Does God exist?' is very different from the question 'Does Energy exist?' I don't mean merely that the questions are different like the question 'Is there any milk?' is different from 'Is there any wine?' Those questions are very unlike because milk is very unlike wine. But they are very like in the sort of procedure which settles them; that is, the logic of milk is like the logic of wine. But surely the way we know of the existence of energy is very different from the way, if any, in which we know of the existence of God. For one thing, people have spoken of knowing the presence of God not from looking around them but from their own hearts. The logic of God may be more like the logic of Energy or of Life than at first appears but surely it is very different.

She: It *is* different. One can't expect to bring out the idiosyncrasies in what you call 'the logic of God' by a single comparison. The way in which we know God Who has been called 'the Soul of the World', 'the Mind of the Universe', might also be compared with the way one knows the soul or mind of another creature. It is clear that one couldn't find the soul behind the face of one's neighbour or one's cat as one could find at last the elusive and even ghostly inhabitant of the house next door. Because of this people have said that when we speak of the consciousness of another this is a way of speaking of those sequences of bodily events which are the manifestations of consciousness, just as when we speak of energy that is a way of speaking of the manifestations of energy and when we speak of a procession that is just a way of speaking of what makes up the procession. Here again this comparison is dangerous unless it is accompanied by a warning. For it neglects the fact that though one who has never tasted what is bitter or sweet and has never felt pain may know very well the behaviour characteristic of, for instance, pain, he yet cannot know pain nor even that another is in pain—not in the way he could had he himself felt pain. It is from looking round him that a man knows of the pain, of the love and of the hate in the world, but it is also from his own heart.

He: Yes, but what I mean is this. Even though we couldn't see energy because it isn't the sort of thing which could be seen we know very well what to look for in order to know of its existence and where it flows, we can measure it and deduce the laws of its transmission and conservation. Even when we ask of someone, 'Is he really pleased to see us?' we know what to look for to prove that the answer is 'Yes,' and what to look for to prove that the answer is 'No.' We may ask him and beg him to tell us the truth, and if we are not satisfied we may await developments, watch for further signs, and these may, in your words, approach more and more a demonstration. But with the questions 'Does God exist?' 'Is this what He approves or that?' there is no agreement as to what to look for, no agreement as to what the character of the order of events must be to count in favour of the answer 'Yes' or in favour of the answer 'No.'

She: Not *no* agreement. If there were *no* agreement that *would* make the question meaningless. But it is not true that there is no agreement. One could describe a future for the world which were it to come would prove the triumph of the Devil. Hells, it is true, are more easily described than Heavens, and Paradise lost than Paradise regained. Descriptions of heaven are apt to be either extremely hazy or to involve too much music or too much hunting. And this isn't a joke, it may spell a contradiction in perfection. But it's not true that we haven't a clue about the kingdom of heaven. Every description of what appears to be heaven and turns out to be hell makes plainer the boundaries of heaven. We don't know what would be heaven and this shows itself in the fluctuating logic of heaven, that is to say in our feeble grasp of what it is we do want to do with the words, 'Will the kingdom of heaven come?' 'Does God exist?' But this doesn't prove that there isn't anything we want to do with them. An artist may not know what he wants to do, and only come to know by doing first one thing which isn't what he wanted to do and then another which also isn't what he wanted to do. But this doesn't prove that there wasn't anything he wanted to do. On the contrary in finding what he didn't want to do he may find at last what he did. In the same way with words, finding out what one didn't mean, one may find out at last what one did mean.

Now with regard to God and the Devil and whether there is any meaning in asking whether they exist: Freud so far from thinking these questions meaningless says in the last of the New Introductory Lectures: 'It seems not to be true that there

is a power in the universe which watches over the well-being
of every individual with parental care and brings all his concerns to a happy ending. On the contrary, the destinies of man
are incompatible with a universal principle of benevolence or
with—what is to some degree contradictory—a universal
principle of justice. Earthquakes, floods and fires do not
differentiate between the good and devout man and the sinner
and unbeliever. And, even if we leave inanimate nature out of
the account and consider the destinies of individual men in so
far as they depend on their relations with others of their own
kind, it is by no means the rule that virtue is rewarded and
wickedness punished, but it happens often enough that the violent, the crafty and the unprincipled seize the desirable goods
of the earth for themselves, while the pious go empty away.
Dark, unfeeling and unloving powers determine human
destiny . . . ' Something about the facts, Freud feels, is brought
out by saying not merely that often men do evil things but
by saying too that 'dark, unfeeling and unloving powers
determine human destiny.' It's preposterous but we know what
he means—not clearly, but obscurely. Others have spoken in
the same way. St. Paul says, 'that which I do I allow not: for
what I would that I do not; but what I hate, that do I.'
Euripides makes Helen say to Menelaus:

> . . . And yet how strange it is!
> I ask not thee; I ask my own sad thought,
> What was there in my heart, that I forgot
> My home and land and all I loved, to fly
> With a strange man? Surely it was not I,
> But Cypris there!

He: It's all very well for her to say, 'It was not I.' The fact is
she did it.

She: There is evasion in such words as there has been ever since
Eve said, 'The serpent beguiled me,' ever since Adam said,
'The woman that thou gavest me she gave me of the tree.'
There is an evasion and confusion and inappropriate humility
perhaps in one who says, 'Yet not I but the grace of God that
dwelleth in me.' And yet is it all evasion and confusion? Is it
for nothing that we speak of someone as not having been himself, as never having been able to be himself. We speak of

compulsive acts, compulsive thought, of having been possessed. Possessed by what? A demon evil or good or both good and evil. And why do we speak so? Because we come on something done by Dr. Jekyll which is out of order, out of character, inexplicable, if it was Dr. Jekyll who was in control. It is in an effort to understand, to bring order into the apparently chaotic, that we find ourselves saying preposterously, 'It wasn't really Dr. Jekyll, it was Mr. Hyde—or the Devil himself.'

He: But there is no need to speak of the Devil here. It is just that there was more in Dr. Jekyll than appeared.

She: Not just that. There was more than there appeared in the man who called about the gas meter and left with the pearls. But that's different. *We* were taken aback when we found he'd gone with the pearls, but *he* wasn't. It was all in order as far as he was concerned. But in those cases of multiple personality, for example in that case Dr. Morton Prince studied, the one personality, Miss Beauchamp, was horrified to learn of the lies which Sally, the other personality, told. Miss Beauchamp couldn't have told such lies and still be Miss Beauchamp.

He: Yes, but Sally was just a part of Miss Beauchamp's unconscious. There were in her desires and thoughts which she didn't allow, as St. Paul says, which she didn't know, to translate St.Paul's Greek still more literally.

She: I am not denying that we can explain the seemingly inexplicable and grasp the order in what seems like chaos with the help of the conceptions of the unconscious, of the Super-ego, of the id, of internal objects, of ghosts that are gone whenever we turn to see them, of currents hidden in the depths of the soul. But if the logic of God and of the Devil is more eccentric than it seems, so also is the logic of the Super-Ego and the Id and the Unconscious. Indeed what makes us speak of the unconscious and the good and the evil in it, the wine of life and the poison of death so mixed, is closely connected with what makes us speak of a hidden power for good—God—and a hidden power for evil—the Devil. For when we speak of the thoughts and acts of Mr. So-and-So as 'coming out of his unconscious' we are often inclined to say that they are not altogether his, that he is compelled, driven, helped, possessed by something not himself. When we recognize the unconscious in the soul we no longer find adequate the model of objects with definite shapes, and we begin to think of the soul as the energy continually flowing and transformed. For example Natasha in *War and Peace* though she loves Prince André Bolkonsky is fascinated by Prince Kouragine. His fast horses stand at the gate and it is nothing in her that prevents her flying with him. It was after Bolkonsky had heard of all this that his friend Peter Bezukov visited him and told him that Natasha was very ill. Bolkonsky replied that he was sorry to hear of her illness and—Tolstoy says—an evil smile like his father's curled his pinched lips. He said, 'Then Prince Kouragine did not after all consent to give her his hand.' Peter replied, 'He could not—he is already married.' Prince André laughed evilly—again reminding one of his father.

Here I feel the presence of evil, evil that has flowed from the father to the son. Anger against Natasha was justified if you like. But that's not what I am now thinking about. Whether anger was or was not justified—in that laugh we feel evil, an evil that we can't place altogether in Prince André. We feel inclined to trace it also to his father. But then when we come to the father it doesn't seem to lie altogether in him either. He was the man who a little before he died accused the daughter who loved him of 'endless imaginary crimes, loaded her with the bitterest reproaches, accused her of having poisoned his existence . . . dismissed her from his presence, saying she might do whatever she pleased, that he would have nothing more to say to her, and that he never would set eyes on her again.' And this was only the climax of what had gone on for years. This wasn't out of character. Or *was* it? For later he is dying. He makes a desperate effort to speak. 'I'm always thinking of you' he says, and as she bows her head to hide her tears he strokes her hair and says, 'I called you all night.' 'If I had but known,' she says. Dark, unfeeling, and unloving powers determine human destiny.

Or is this going too far? Is it evil and unloving power only that determines human destiny and directs the course of nature? Or is there also at work a good and loving power? It has been said that once at least a higher gift than grace did flesh and blood refine, God's essence and his very self—in the body of Jesus. Whether this statement is true or false is not now the point but whether it's so obscure as to be senseless. Obscure undoubtedly it is but senseless it is not, beyond the scope of reason it is not. For to say that in Nero God was incarnate is not to utter a senseless string of words nor merely to express a surprising sentiment; it is to make a statement which is absurd because it is against all reason. If I say of a cat, 'This cat is an abracadabra' I utter a senseless string of words, I don't make a statement at all and therefore don't make an absurd statement. But if I say of a cat which is plainly dead, 'In this cat there is life' I make a statement which is absurd because it is against all reason. The cat is not hunting, eating, sleeping, breathing; it is stiff and cold. In the same way the words, 'In Nero God was incarnate' are not without any meaning; one who utters them makes a statement, he makes a statement which is absurd and *against* all reason and therefore *not* beyond the scope of reason. Now if a statement is not beyond the scope of reason then any logically parallel statement is also not beyond the scope of reason. For example, the statement, 'Your house is well designed' is not beyond the scope of reason. It may be obviously true or absurdly false or obviously neither true nor false, but it's not beyond the scope of reason. The statement, 'My house is well designed' is logically parallel to the statement, 'Your house is well designed.' The statement, 'My house is well designed' may be absurdly false or neither true nor false or obviously true. But like the parallel statement about your house it is not beyond the scope of reason. The statement 'In Jesus God was incarnate' is logically parallel to 'In Nero God was incarnate.' The latter we noticed is not beyond the scope of reason. Therefore the statement 'In Jesus God was incarnate' is not beyond the scope of reason.

And we may come at the same result more directly. Consider the words 'Was there someone, Jesus, in whom God was incarnate?' These words call first for investigation. Was there such a person as Jesus is alleged to have been? Was there someone born of a virgin? Was there someone who rose from the dead? Was there someone who said all or some or most of the things Jesus is alleged to have said? Did someone speak as this man is said to have spoken? These things settled, we have only started. How far does the rest of experience show that what this man said was true? Did what

Jesus said reveal what we hadn't known or what we had known but hadn't recognized? Was there someone, Jesus, who was God incarnate? The question calls for investigation but it also calls like every other question for thought, reflection, reason. He made himself the Son of God. 'Preposterous presumption' the priests said, but was it the truth? The facts agreed upon, still a question is before the bar of reason as when, the facts agreed upon, still a question comes before a court. 'Was there negligence or was there not?' To such a question maybe the answer is 'Yes,' maybe the answer is 'No,' maybe the answer is neither 'Yes' nor 'No.' But the question is not beyond the scope of reason. On the contrary it calls for very careful consideration and not the less when what's relevant is conflicting and not the less because what's relevant is not enumerable because there's not a separate name for every relevant feature of the case and an index to measure its weight. In a cat crouched to spring burns the flame of life. There are signs we can mention—nothing moves but, very slightly, the tail and there's something about the eyes but what? She springs. Still the proof of life eludes language but it's there, was there, and will be there, in the moving picture before us. Was Jesus God incarnate? The law in this matter is not as simple nor as definite nor as fully written out in statutes as we might wish it could be. The question is large, slippery, subtle. But it is not true that nothing is more relevant to it than another, so that nothing supports one answer more than it supports the other. On the contrary every incident in the life of Christ is relevant to this question as every incident in the life of Nero is relevant to the same question about him. To both much more is relevant. For an affirmative answer to either implies the existence of God. And to this question every incident in the history of the world is relevant—whether it is the fall of a sparrow or the coming of harvest, the passing of an empire or the fading of a smile.

Here ends this talk about how in the end questions about God and the Devil are to be answered.

The statement 'There is someone who feeds the cattle upon a thousand hills, who can match the powers of evil and lift up the everlasting doors' is not one to which what is still hidden from us in space and time is all irrelevant. But it seems to me it is not only this that makes the question, 'Is that statement true?' a hard one. It is also the fact that this question calls upon us to consider all that is already before us, in case it should happen that having eyes we see not, and having ears we hear not.

The consideration this question calls for cannot be conducted by a definite step by step procedure like that of one who calculates the height or weight or prospects of life of the average man or the Bengal tiger. Nor is it a question which though it has no answer 'Yes' or 'No' may yet be considered on perfectly conventional lines like the question before the court 'Was there or was there not neglect of duty?' For the statement 'There is one above who gives order and life amongst disorder and death' when taken on perfectly conventional lines is as preposterous as the statement that the sun doesn't move though we see it climb the sky. Nor are the new lines on which the statement is to be taken firmly fixed as they are with 'We are turning to the sun at n m.p.h.' And yet in spite of all this and whatever the answer may be the old question 'Does God exist?' 'Does the Devil exist'? aren't senseless, aren't beyond the scope of thought and reason. On the contrary they call for new awareness of what has so long been about us, in case knowing nature so well we never know her.

Nothing in all this makes less of the call for critical attention, whatever sort of statement we are considering. Nothing in all this makes less of the need to get clear about what we mean by a statement, to get clear as to what we are comparing with what. Just this is called for, just this done, in that statement so obvious yet so preposterous, 'My dear, it's the Taj Mahal.'

II

Freewill

A When a person is criticized for having done this or that, before we can be sure that the criticism is justified we have to make sure of the facts. We have to make sure that he did what he is alleged to have done and also in what circumstances he did it. What is more, the facts ascertained, we need to consider them. Sometimes this is easy and hardly takes a moment but sometimes it is far from easy.

B Nobody denies this.

A As you say, nobody denies this. Those philosophers who have tried to describe what it is that we do when we concern ourselves with a question as to whether a person acted wrongly or rightly have never denied that in order to answer such a question we must ascertain the facts. Those who like Hume and more modern writers have emphasized how much our feelings are involved in moral judgement have not denied that our feelings towards a man because of what he has done may be quite changed when we learn more of the circumstances. Those who have spoken of 'the voice of conscience', 'the moral sense' and 'the moral intuition', telling us, showing us, making plain to us, what is wrong or right, have never pretended that these faculties operate without our learning the circumstances in which a thing was done. The halo that surrounds the head of a saint does not become visible till we know he has paid the rent.

But both those who have said that once the facts are ascertained then moral judgement is a matter for the sentiments, for the feelings, because then reason has no more room to operate, and those who have said that once the facts are ascertained then moral judgement is a matter for intuition and not for reasoning have obscured or distorted the character of what we do when, the facts well known, we still need a

C

moment to consider things, time to think them over, and again think them over.

B   How do you mean?

A   Well to say that when a question arises between oneself and another, or in one's own mind, as to whether someone was all that bad in what he did, then, once the facts are ascertained, there is no room for reason, does suggest that when the facts are known it's useless to argue, ridiculous to reason.

B   But isn't it? You can't prove an act wrong or right, can you? I mean you can of course prove to someone that he was mistaken about what happened and what was done but can you show that what was done was wrong or right?

A   Didn't Christ with his very obvious story of the good Samaritan show us something about what we might easily do or not do in much less obvious cases? And in *Crime and Punishment* Raskolnikov knew what happened on the night he took the axe to the pawnbroker. He knew the circumstances. He knew it all. But he took some time to think it over—to think over the matter of whether he was an innocent as he had told himself or as guilty as he felt himself. Like K in Kafka's *The Trial*, we know as well as any tribunal our own biographies, but, like him, we are very much concerned to hear argument upon our case. The trial is not always conducted in a satisfactory manner. Counsel for the defence shouts, counsel for the prosecution will whisper. And then too, a verdict is never reached. Only God knows the verdict. He at any time may write it on the wall. But this is because he not only knows each item in the infinite account but has at all times weighed them in the unerring balances of the divine judgement.

B   I see what you mean. You mean that just as in cases in the courts even when the facts are known it is necessary to hear argument before answering such questions as 'Was there negligence or was there not?' 'Was it fair comment or was it not?' so even when the facts are known, it is necessary to hear argument before answering such questions as 'Was he or wasn't he such a blackguard, and *how* was he a blackguard?'

A   Exactly so.

B   And I quite agree with you. But I thought you were going to say something about the freedom of the will. And I don't see what all this has got to do with that.

A When a man is blamed, or, for that matter, when he is praised, for what he did or did not do, one of the things we need to find out and one of the things we need to consider, is whether and how far he could have acted differently. For instance, suppose I say to you in tones which betray some contempt 'And you did nothing to stop all this', then you may reply 'I did nothing. But then I was bound hand and foot'. Again you may say to me 'Well that speaks well for him. You say he kept working on the combination though he knew the place might blow up at any time' then—I may reply 'Yes but he hadn't much choice. A six gun at his back kept his fingers busy'.

B All that sort of talk seems quite proper and reasonable. What is it you want to say about it?

A Such explanations are very reasonable and proper. We may in this or that instance question the conclusion 'He couldn't help himself' but we don't reckon such explanations beside the point. For example, someone excuses another with the words 'Well but he was drunk'. We may reply 'Exactly, he was drunk. "In vino veritas", they say'. But we don't count his being drunk beside the point. It may not reduce the blame. It may increase it. But it alters the quality of it.

B Certainly, obviously. Is this all you wanted to say?

A No. I wanted to understand those who have said '*No-one* can *ever* help doing what he does'.

B Now that is staggering. That in fact is preposterous.

A And yet it seems it must be right. Today your car refuses to start although it always starts so readily. There seems no explanation but of course really there is. Usually you are in good spirits but today you are depressed. There seems no explanation. But there is. Whatever happens, whether it is the fall of leaves on water or of eyelashes on cheeks, it wouldn't have the significance it has were it not in a causal network that links before and after. In short, there's always a reason why. And that's why people have said 'Every event, every feature of every event is determined; so every action, every choice is determined and again determined. And if it is determined it isn't free'.

B But what does this mean—'Every event is determined'? All it means is that there is always an explanation, always a reason why. And that doesn't imply that nothing ever acts freely. When we say of a mechanism that it is now running freely while before it was not we do not mean that there is no explanation for its running as it's now running while there was an explanation for its running as it did. When we say 'He was free in the matter, she was not' we do not mean that there is an explanation for why she acted as she did but no explanation for why he acted as he did.

A But surely we think of a human being who runs to help another as acting freely, as having been free to do something different, in a way in which a machine doesn't act freely however freely it runs. Surely we think of human beings as having a freedom which machines have not. Now can we be right in thinking this if all human action is no less explicable, no less part of a causal network, than the action of machines?

B Certainly a man who runs to help another acts freely in a way a machine does not. Human beings choose. Machines don't. Animals choose only in a rudimentary way. A man who is paralysed may sit in a wheeled chair while another drowns. He is not bound by bonds or overwhelmed by waves. But he has no choice in the matter. He hasn't the freedom of action of one who is not paralysed. But when we say of someone that in doing what he has done he acted freely, that he could have done something different, that he had a choice in the matter, we do not mean that there is no explanation for the fact that he chose as he did and acted as he did.

A I see that now. But surely even when a person has a choice he or she is not always quite free. I mean suppose a woman has married a man she ought never to have married. It may be true that she could have married someone else had she chosen to do so and yet be true that she was not quite free to do so. For it may be that before her marriage she said to her mother 'I think I'll marry Jack'—Jack being the man she didn't marry—and that her mother then said to her 'Well dear, of course your father and I leave you entirely free in this momentous decision but ... I had hoped ... but there I suppose old people ... ' and so on.

B I did not say that when we consider whether a person in acting as she or he did acted freely, we are concerned only with whether she or he had some choice in the matter or no choice. Often we are concerned with what sort of choice she or he had.

A We are. For the light or shadow which a person's action or inaction throws upon his character depends not merely on whether there is something else he could have done but on what else he could have done. If a girl's parents would be distressed if she married a certain man it is still open to her to marry him but it is not open to her to marry him without their being distressed. If in these circumstances she refuses his offer of marriage this throws a light upon her character but not that light it would have thrown, had circumstances left her more freedom in the matter.

When we ask whether or how far a person acted freely in doing what she or he did we want to know, we want to consider, the circumstances. For we want to see that person for what she or he is.

B Exactly. That is what we are concerned with. We are not concerned with whether or no there was *some* explanation for what she or he did. That is why I say that to argue from the fact that there is always some explanation for what a man does to the conclusion that no-one is ever free in what he does is to argue confusedly, badly. What is more it is to reach a conclusion which is false. For every day there happens all that needs to happen to prove that though sometimes a person has little or no choice in what he or she does or does not do at other times he is as free as a bird in summer air, as free as a man on a ship which will sail as near the wind as he could wish.

A I have been thinking over what you said and I agree that such words as 'No-one ever acts freely' or 'No-one ever could have done anything different from what he did do,' carry the suggestion that whenever one says of someone that he was, on a certain occasion, free to do something different from what he did then one is wrong. And I agree that that suggestion is false. But it now seems to me that one who says 'No-one really ever acts freely' may have no wish to convey this false suggestion. He may wish to convey something different, something which is, I think, well worth our attention.

B Do you mean that whenever someone says 'No-one ever

acts freely' or 'Really no-one ever acts freely' he never wants to convey what his words naturally suggest but always something different which his words do not naturally suggest?

A   No I don't mean that. On the contrary I remember that in our last discussion I was at first more than half inclined to suggest that whenever in everyday life we say such a thing as 'She didn't marry him although she was quite free to do so' we are mistaken. I admit that that is what I meant to suggest when I said 'It seems it must be true that no-one ever acts freely.' I did not have in mind some more recondite suggestion. I meant to make the suggestion which my words very naturally conveyed. And I admit that I made this suggestion, this false suggestion, because I was influenced by the confused reasoning I then presented—you will remember that I argued somewhat as follows: Every human action is explicable, every human action is as much a part of a causal network as the behaviour of an animal or the movement of a machine. Therefore every human action is determined. Therefore no human action is free. Therefore nobody ever acts freely.

B   I do remember that. And surely there have been others who have reasoned in a similar way and then made a suggestion which you allow you wished to make and now allow was unfounded and false.

A   I don't deny that. But that leaves it still possible for someone to say 'No-one ever really acts freely' without reasoning in this way and without wishing to suggest that whenever we say of someone 'He went of his own free will' we are mistaken. A person who says 'No-one ever really acts freely' may wish to put before us not what his words first suggest to us but something more recondite.

B   Of course it is possible. But why should he use a form of words which naturally suggests what he does not want to suggest? Surely he would do better to use words which at once suggest what he does want to suggest?

A   As you know, it sometimes happens that a person wants to convey what no words available at the time will quickly and unmistakably convey. He may then be forgiven for using words which at first convey only a hint of what he means and may suggest what he does not mean. For instance, imagine a time when scientific knowledge is very rudimentary. A man is washing a carriage. He jacks up one wheel and sets it spinning. Although he has often done this before he is now struck by the fact that the wheel though it isn't touching the ground and isn't hindered by mud or water or brakes slows down and stops. He asks himself 'Why does it stop when there is nothing to stop it?' and then he answers his own question by saying 'There is something to stop it—air. And air is like water.' But now if this philosophical scientist goes about saying 'No wheel on earth ever really turns freely' he is likely to be misunderstood. Other people who still use the words 'moving freely' in the way they always have been used, that is, to distinguish between a wheel or a pendulum which is moving unhindered by anything but air and one which is moving in water or milk or oil, may misunderstand him. Some of them may think that he means that whenever people have distinguished between one thing and another by saying 'This is moving freely, that is not' they have been mistaken. Others may say 'No. He cannot be saying anything which is so plainly false. He has without warning changed the use of words, and when he says "Nothing really moves freely" all he means is that every movement has some explanation'. Both these interpretations are wrong. The philosophical scientist whom we have imagined is neither denying the important differences which have so far been marked by saying 'This is moving freely, that is not' nor asserting merely that for every movement there is some explanation. He is beginning to point out the affinities, the unremarked affinities, between, for example, a wheel turning in the air and a wheel turning in water or milk or oil.

B   And you, I take it, are now suggesting that a person who says 'No-one ever really acts freely' may be one who is not denying the important differences which have so far been marked by saying such things as 'He was quite free in the matter she was not' but is taking a first step towards drawing our attention to certain affinities between some or all of those actions we have so far called 'free' and those we have called 'not free'. I don't say that nobody could do this. I don't say that nobody has done this. But I do ask what affinities this philosophical psychologist is trying to draw attention to by the extravagant words 'No-one ever really acts freely'?

A   There isn't a word for them. That is why he uses the extravagant words he does. I mean, so far as I know there is no
better way of giving in a word or two some hint of what this
philosophical scientist wishes to remark than by saying 'No-
one ever really acts freely' or 'We are all in some degree in
bondage' or something of that sort.

B   And do you mean that if one is unable at once to understand
these paradoxes then there is nothing further to be said to help
one?

A   No, no. Of course not. There is much to be said. Think of
someone who says 'We're all mad really'. He . . .

B   Ah! but that's different. We all by now know more or
less what he means. It's a commonplace.

A   It's true that we now readily accept this statement without
thinking. So much so that on the one hand we may accept it
without recognizing the shocking affinities it calls attention to
while on the other hand we may accept it without retaining
our commonsense recognition of the profound differences it
makes little of. But what I want to say now is that he who first
said 'We are all mad really' spoke extravagantly. And I remember that when as a child I first heard these words I had a
very feeble grasp of what they refer to. What has given me
a better grasp of what they refer to is, no doubt, in part, experience. But words have helped, although I still do not know
some cautious form of words which will do all that is done by the
extravagant and even dangerous formula 'We are all mad'.
Often when we say that words fail us the truth is not that they
fail us but that they will not serve us in the way we had expected of them. They may still be there to give us in other
ways the help we need. Even when it is most true that without
a fresh look at experience words are 'as sounding brass or
a tinkling cymbal' they may yet help one to look again at one's
own experience, to look beyond one's own experience, and to
understand. In spite of all the books which have been written
since Jeremiah wrote 'The heart of man is evil continually and
desperately wicked. Who shall know it'? our knowledge of
ourselves is far from what it might be. We may feel at times that
those who have tried to enlighten us have said only either what
we know already or what is so obscure that we don't know
what is meant.

B Well but now come back to the dark saying that none of us is free. I said that if these words don't mean what they naturally suggest then I don't know what they mean. You said that there isn't a word for it but that words have been found or can be found which in conjunction with a fresh look at experience can help us to cash this portentous statement in the concrete. What are these words?

A I am not an artist. I am not one who can present in the particular all the range of reality which someone else in some general but mystifying statement has tried to illuminate.

B Surely you can say something.

A Of course I can say something. I'll begin with this. You agreed that the girl whom her mother wished to leave quite free in the matter of whom she was to marry was not really left quite free in spite of the fact that she still could have married the man she wished to marry.

B She was blackmailed.

A A rather extravagant description. But I know what you mean. And now we may ask: 'When is there blackmail and when is there not?' 'When is love bondage and when is it freedom?' 'When does a person act of herself or of himself and when not?' When a person is possessed by a devil or by someone else, he cannot be himself. But then how often do we hear in someone's voice the voice of another, see in someone's gesture the gesture of another? Sometimes the voice and gesture are nevertheless his own but sometimes they are not; for sometimes a boy is a soldier because his father was a soldier and he is also a soldier like his father, but sometimes though he makes his life in the army he is never a soldier. Sometimes a man dies without ever having been more than half himself; without having become free. In Marquand's novel, *H. M. Pulham Esq.*, a young man finds in a New York advertising firm a very different life from that he was used to at home and at his school. At the office he meets a man and a woman and he likes them both although the outlook of each of them is very different from his own and that of his family. The woman he comes to want to marry. She feels a difference between them and hesitates. Then his father dies, he returns to his home town and takes up his father's business and marries a girl his family would regard as thoroughly suitable. All goes well, they have two children, they are fond of each other, they are, he insists, happy together. But the story is a subtle study of how far in his life he is himself and how far he never is. Or take Tolstoy's story *The Death of Ivan Ilyitch*. Ivan Ilyitch had been very successful in his life and had been able to do what he wished. Then an illness seized him and it was then that, as Tolstoy says 'It struck him that those scarcely detected impulses of struggle within him against what was considered good by persons of higher position, scarcely detected impulses which he had dismissed, that they might be the real thing, and everything else might be not the right thing. And his official work, and his ordering of his daily life and of his family and these social and official interests—all that might be not the right thing. He tried to defend it all to himself, and suddenly he felt all the weakness of what he was defending. And it was useless to defend it.

'But if it's so, he said to himself, and I am leaving life with the consciousness that I have lost all that was given, and there's no correcting it, then what? He lay on his back and began going over his whole life entirely anew. When he saw the footman in the morning, then his wife, then his daughter, then the doctor, every movement they made, every word they uttered, confirmed for him the terrible truth that had been revealed to him in the night. In them he saw himself, saw all in which he had lived, and saw distinctly that it was all not the right thing; it was a horrible vast deception that concealed both life and death.'

B   I begin to see what you mean. But I must say that this conception of freedom as an ideal to which we seldom or never attain, seems to me very hazy.

A   It is hazy. But that doesn't mean that it's useless or that it is not worth making it clearer. For instance it helps us to understand why Christ said 'Judge not that ye be not judged' and yet on occasion made judgement without mincing words. He called the Pharisees hypocrites.

B   How does it help us?

A   The more we realize how much a man's whole way of life or his action or inaction on a particular occasion may deceive us and him as to his real nature, the more we realize how difficult it is to reach a final judgement, a judgement which takes everything into account and gives it its correct weight. But in the first place this doesn't mean that such a judgement is impossible, that there is no truth to be found, no reality to be seen—not even by one from whom no secrets are hid. And even if it is not in mortals to reach such a judgement that doesn't mean that they cannot make limited judgements, judgements which do not profess to take everything into account and yet are valuable, necessary to us in the hurry, in the business, of life.

B I am not quite clear what you mean.

A The woman taken in adultery had not kept the ten commandments. In that she differed from those who had. This difference does not become illusory if we now begin to take into account other things and ask 'But after all how different in their hearts were those who kept the commandments from the woman who had not'? This question reminds us that we have not taken all things into account. But it leaves it still true that what's in a man's heart is one thing and what he does is another. Christ did not deny that the woman had sinned. He said 'Neither do I condemn thee. Go and sin no more'.

But though we do make and need to make limited judgements we need again and again to call to mind how different they are from the divine judgement in which both easy forgiveness and easy condemnation are impossible. This is the judgement we ask for ourselves. For we ask that at our own trial counsel and judge shall proceed with infinite patience. We ask that they shall not judge a part of the picture without seeing the whole. We ask that they shall consider, ruthlessly but with understanding, circumstance beyond circumstance, wheel within wheel.

Asking for this patience for ourselves we then ask it for others and so ask it of ourselves.

We know that action cannot always wait for such judgement. The law must take its course and rightly the sheriff's men ride hard behind the man who has broken it. But at times his case is such that we take leave to note with a certain satisfaction the unfaltering gait of the good beast that carries him 'beyond the ten commandments'.

III

Existentialism[1]

Professor Kuhn agrees with the Existentialists when like many other 'teachers of humanity' they teach that it is necessary for man to die in order to live. He disagrees with them as to 'the nature of that reality which is to shatter the screens and shelters around us. In Existentialism, crisis is conceived as an encounter with "Nothingness", that is, the privation of meaning and reality, whereas, in truth, it seems to me that it is the incomprehensible fullness of meaning and reality, God alone, who is the rightful claimant to the role of the saving destroyer. The Existentialists take the road to Calvary, but arriving there they find the place empty except for two thieves dying on their crosses' (pp. x, xi). (It should here be recalled that there are Existentialists who call themselves Christians and Christians who call themselves Existentialists. But then if one were to put into the picture of an Existentialist only features found in every Existentialist the result would not be much like an Existentialist.) (Here see p. 103.)

In Chapter I, Professor Kuhn explains the Existentialists' use of 'exists'. 'We take an interest in the existence of the penny in our pocket or in the non-existence of the world. But, the Existentialist asks, are not these manifold and changing interests rooted in one basic and persistent interest—the interest which man takes in his own existence? This being so, we are justified in ascribing existence in a more specific sense to that being which in existing is infinitely concerned about his existence. For it is true that the meaning though not the fact of the difference between existence and non-existence of things other

---

[1] *Encounter with Nothingness. An Essay on Existentialism.* Helmut Kuhn, Professor of Philosophy at Erlangen University. London. Methuen & Co. Ltd. xxii + 147. pp. 8s. 6d.

than man is derived from, or at any rate elucidated by, man's passionate interest in his own existence or his equally passionate fear of annihilation' (p. 4). This explanation of a new meaning of 'exists' is, for me, still inadequate. What is it to be concerned about one's own existence? Is it merely to wish to live? No, see p. 61. Is it to wish to have a life that isn't 'meaningless'? And are we to say that a stick or a stone exists only in so far as it ministers to the meaning of Life?

In Chapter II Professor Kuhn reviews the sources of Existentialism. Chapter III is on the experience of estrangement. Here Plato, Paul, Kant, Hegel, Kierkegaard, Kafka, Marx, Heidegger, Sartre, T. S. Eliot and others are set side by side and, in spite of the brevity of the treatment, we feel something of the desperateness of man's endeavour to find in what seems a waste land signs that it is not.

Professor Kuhn disagrees with those who regard Existentialism as an ephemeral fashion. 'The Existentialist claims to initiate us, through acquaintance with Nothingness, into the maturity of disillusionment. This claim faithfully expresses a thought latent in the deeds and events which compose our contemporary world' (p. xiv). But more—Existentialism 're-affirms a universal truth about man. Man must purchase victory at the price of an ultimate defeat. But the grave question before us is whether Existentialism interprets this law of crisis correctly'.

In Chapter IV, Subjective Truth, we get an impression of how Existentialists use in a muddled way muddled metaphysics to give misery a more imposing appearance. But if the muddle is to be exposed the exposition of it must be itself less muddled. In Chapter V, Gravediggers at Work, Professor Kuhn says that the Existentialist deserves praise for repudiating the rationalist construction of man as a 'thinking thing' (*res cogitans*) and recalling to us that concrete whole which everyone of us is (p. 70), but urges that 'he mars his discovery by overlooking or rejecting three metaphysical (*sic*) concepts which alone could make it fruitful: the idea of contemplation, the idea of love and the idea of rational faith'. This chapter deserves the most serious attention. So do those that follow. Chapter VI is concerned with the passage through 'acute despair' necessary to the conquest of 'latent despair'. 'When the Existentialist (or, I would add, some incident of life)

shows the abyss, we are startled. But at the bottom of our minds
we may also feel that we knew all this before, that we had been
standing at the brink of the abyss all our life and we dared not
confess it' (p. xiv). It suddenly seems as if 'everything happens
and nothing matters'. Out of this may come frantic action—
for 'there is an active tedium just as there is a passive one'
(p. 96), or inaction in which anguish has changed into a longing
for death (p. xvi). Or again anguish may lead (Sartre, Bertrand Russell in *A Free Man's Worship*) to an attempt to feel at
home in anguish and nothingness (p. 94). Or (Marcel), it may
be said that *ennui* arises from an initial error and that 'I need
only rise to those concrete experiences of participation through
which the presence of my fellow man as a "thou" rather than
a mere "he" is revealed to me, together with my own presence
to myself, and finally to the presence of God . . . in order to . . .
rejoin the inexhaustible plenitude of Being' (p. 95). The last
chapters are called The Crisis of the Drama, Illumination
through Anguish and Beyond Crisis. I cannot give even a
summary here. On p. 158 it is argued that an Existentialist
cannot consistently say that freedom does not involve irre-
sponsibility and that the individual's freedom limits itself through
his being with others. I do not follow this argument.

The metaphysics in this book, for example the discussion of
objective truth (pp. 44 and 66), seems to me sketchy and slippery.

And the Existentialist's argument for despair outlined on
p. xiii needs a much more critical examination. The Existentialist is, not unfairly I think, represented as asking, 'What do
you will with unwavering devotion, so that everything else is
willed and lived only for the sake of this first objective and great-
est good?' (We are reminded of St. Augustine's words, 'the
chief good—that which will leave us nothing further to seek
in order to be blessed, if only we make all our actions refer to
it . . . ' (*City of God*, Book viii. 8.) The Existentialist is represented as answering with a string of negations 'not the promotion
of what belongs in the field of my professional duties; not
wife, children and friends; not wealth, learning or power; not
higher living standards for all men; not. . . '

Suppose it is true that no one of these things is sufficient to
make life meaningful. It does not follow that life is not meaningful. Suppose further that it is true that no one of these things is

necessary to life's having a meaning. It does not follow that life hasn't a meaning nor even that it isn't these things which give it its meaning. After all no one of a horse's legs suffices to keep him standing up, and at the blacksmith's it is demonstrated that no leg is indispensable for his standing up, but of course this doesn't mean that no horse stands up nor that he stands up on anything but his own legs. To win a set at tennis is not the *summum bonum* but this doesn't prove that it is not *part* of what makes *a* life good. Maybe in Heaven they don't play tennis or make war. Maybe a world in which there is so much defeat and death is not worth the money. But if so it's not because it's nothing to the good to have what it takes to win when all seems lost—whether at Wimbledon or Stalingrad.

Saints and cynics alike too readily assume it agreed that birds, beasts, flowers and fast cars have nothing to do with the case or at any rate that they aren't good enough. It is true that even friends sometimes sadly disappoint one another, but ... However there is no space to argue the matter here. Only, as Solomon remarked, a dish of herbs is under certain circumstances better than much grander food, though those circumstances are of infinite subtlety.

Nevertheless, this small book on the 'Encounter with Nothingness' seems to me good. It is sympathetic and serious and in it learning is used to bring together into illuminating conjunction the thoughts of great thinkers. I especially like its challenge to those who sometimes write as if cheerfulness *must* arise from intellectual inadequacy or dishonesty, stupidity or evasion. Anguish can be 'adulterated with longing for death' (p. xvi). When I read Existentialist writings I sometimes have an uncomfortable feeling that here in what I am reading is evasion. As Professor Kuhn says, Existentialists face what many human beings, for good or ill, don't face. But they do so only up to a point—after all one of the best ways of keeping concealed the most horrible is to emphasize the horror of the less horrible and to denigrate the good. Freud has a good deal to say about despair. But Existentialists and writers about Existentialists say very little about Freud. Why? There are no short cuts to honest optimism but nor are there to honest pessimism.

IV

The Meanings of the Questions of Life

When one asks 'What is the meaning of life?' one begins to wonder whether this large, hazy and bewildering question itself has any meaning. Some people indeed have said boldly that the question has no meaning. I believe this is a mistake. But it is a mistake which is not without excuse. And I hope that by examining the excuse we may begin to remedy the mistake, and so come to see that whether or not life has a meaning it is not senseless to enquire whether it has or not. First, then, what has led some people to think that the whole enquiry is senseless?

There is an old story which runs something like this: A child asked an old man 'What holds up the world? What holds up all things?' The old man answered 'A giant'. The child asked 'And what holds up the giant? You must tell me what holds up the giant'. The old man answered 'An elephant'. The child said, 'And what holds up the elephant?' The old man answered 'A tortoise'. The child said 'You still have not told me what holds up all things. For what holds up the tortoise'. The old man answered 'Run away and don't ask me so many questions'.

From this story we can see how it may happen that a question which looks very like sensible meaningful questions may turn out to be a senseless, meaningless one. Again and again when we ask 'What supports this?' it is possible to give a sensible answer. For instance what supports the top-most card in a house of cards? The cards beneath it which are in their turn supported by the cards beneath them. What supports all the cards? The table. What supports the table? The floor and the earth. But the question 'What supports all things, absolutely all things?' is different. It is absurd, it is senseless, like the question 'What is bigger than the largest thing in the world?' And it is easy to see why the question 'What supports all things?' is absurd. Whenever we ask, 'What supports thing A or these things A, B, C', then we can answer this question only by mentioning some thing other than the thing A or things A, B, C about which we are asked 'What supports it or them'. We must if we are to answer the question mention something D other than those things which form the subject of our question, and we must say that this thing is what supports them. If we mean by the phrase 'all things' absolutely all things which exist then obviously there is nothing outside that about which we are now asked 'What supports all this?' Consequently any answer to the question will be self-contradictory just as any answer to the question 'What is bigger than the biggest of all things' must be self-contradictory. Such questions are absurd, or, if you like, silly and senseless.

In a like way again and again when we ask 'What is the meaning of this?' we answer in terms of something other than this. For instance imagine that there has been a quarrel in the street. One man is hitting another man on the jaw. A policeman hurries up. 'Now then' he says, 'what is the meaning of all this?' He wants to know what led up to the quarrel, what caused it. It is no good saying to the policeman 'It's a quarrel'. He knows there is a quarrel. What he wants to know is what went before the quarrel, what led up to it. To answer him we must mention something other than the quarrel itself. Again suppose a man is driving a motor car and sees in front of him a road sign, perhaps a red flag, perhaps a skull and cross bones. 'What does this mean?' he asks and when he asks this he wants to know what the sign points to. To answer we must mention something other than the sign itself, such as a dangerous corner in the road. Imagine a doctor sees an extraordinary rash on the face of his patient. He is astonished and murmurs to himself 'What is the meaning of this?'. He wants to know what caused the strange symptoms, or what they will lead to, or both. In any case in order to answer his question he must find something which went before or comes after and lies outside that about which he asks 'What does this mean?'. This need to look before or after in order to answer a question of the sort 'What is the meaning of this?' is so common, so characteristic, a feature of

D

such questions that it is natural to think that when it is impossible to answer such a question in this way then the question has no sense. Now what happens when we ask 'What is the meaning of life?'

Perhaps someone here replies, the meaning, the significance of this present life, this life on earth, lies in a life hereafter, a life in heaven. All right. But imagine that some persistent enquirer asks, 'But what I am asking is what is the meaning of all life, life here and life beyond, life now and life hereafter? What is the meaning of all things in earth and heaven?' Are we to say that this question is absurd because there cannot be anything beyond all things while at the same time any answer to 'What is the meaning of all things?' must point to some thing beyond all things?

Imagine that we come into a theatre after a play has started and are obliged to leave before it ends. We may then be puzzled by the part of the play that we are able to see. We may ask 'What does it mean?'. In this case we want to know what went before and what came after in order to understand the part we saw. But sometimes even when we have seen and heard a play from the beginning to the end we are still puzzled and still ask what does the whole thing mean. In this case we are not asking what came before or what came after, we are not asking about anything outside the play itself. We are, if you like asking a very different sort of question from that we usually put with the words 'What does this mean?' But we are still asking a real question, we are still asking a question which has sense and is not absurd. For our words express a wish to grasp the character, the significance of the whole play. They are a confession that we have not yet done this and they are a request for help in doing it. Is the play a tragedy, a comedy or a tale told by an idiot? The pattern of it is so complex, so bewildering, our grasp of it still so inadequate, that we don't know what to say, still less whether to call it good or bad. But this question is not senseless.

In the same way when we ask 'what is the meaning of all things?' we are not asking a senseless question. In this case, of course, we have not witnessed the whole play, we have only an idea in outline of what went before and what will come after that small part of history which we witness. But with the words 'What is the meaning of it all?' we are trying to find the order in the drama of Time. The question may be beyond us. A child may be able to understand, to grasp a simple play and be unable to understand and grasp a play more complex and more subtle. We do not say on this account that when he asks of the larger more complex play 'What does it mean?' then his question is senseless, nor even that it is senseless for him. He has asked and even answered such a question in simpler cases, he knows the sort of effort, the sort of movement of the mind which such a question calls for, and we do not say that a question is meaningless to him merely because he is not yet able to carry out quite successfully the movement of that sort which is needed in order to answer a complex question of that sort. We do not say that a question in mathematics which is at present rather beyond us is meaningless to us. We know the type of procedure it calls for and may make efforts which bring us nearer and nearer to an answer. We are able to find the meaning which lies not outside but within very complex but still limited wholes whether these are dramas of art or of real life. When we ask 'What is the meaning of all things?' we are bewildered and have not that grasp of the order of things the desire for which we express when we ask that question. But this does not render the question senseless nor make it impossible for us to move towards an answer.

We must however remember that what one calls answering such a question is not giving an answer. I mean we cannot answer such a question in the form: 'The meaning is this'.

Such an idea about what form answering a question must take may lead to a new despair in which we feel we cannot do anything in the way of answering such a question as 'What is the meaning in it all?' merely because we are not able to sum up our results in a phrase or formula.

When we ask what is the meaning of this play or this picture we cannot express the understanding which this question may lead to in the form of a list of just those things in the play or the picture which give it its meaning. No. The meaning eludes such a list. This does not mean that words quite fail us. They may yet help us provided that we do not expect of them more than they can do.

A person who is asked what he finds so hateful or so lovable in another may with words help himself and us in grasping what it is that so moves him. But he will only mislead us and himself if he pretends that his words are a complete account of all that there is in the matter.

It is the same when we ask what is it in all things that makes it all so good, so bad, so grand, so contemptible. We must not anticipate that the answer can be given in a word or in a neat list. But this does not mean that we can do nothing towards answering these questions nor even that words will not help us. Indeed surely the historians, the scientists, the prophets, the dramatists and the poets have said much which may help any man who asks himself: Is the drama of time meaningless as a tale told by an idiot? Or is it not meaningless? And if it is not meaningless is it a comedy or a tragedy, a triumph or a disaster, or is it a mixture in which sweet and bitter are for ever mixed?

V

Religious Belief

The recently-published book, *New Essays in Philosophical Theology*, seems to me very good.[1] Flew presents clearly yet sympathetically the difficulty he finds in what is said by men of religion. Mitchell and Crombie (see perhaps especially p. 124) honestly try to meet that difficulty. Hare's answer (p. 49) seems to me seriously confused. He appears to put under the same heading, 'one who has a *blik*', (a) the plain man who in the light of experience very reasonably believes in steel, (b) the metaphysician who insists that the plain man 'really' has no reason to believe in steel, (c) the madman who insists that everyone is against him, (d) the religious person who insists that there is One who is for him. McPherson (p. 131), though he warns us against assuming that a statement is senseless when it is not amenable to examination on the lines one might expect, seems to me to encourage the idea that a belief is not rational when the reasons for it cannot be stated in words. However, there is elsewhere in this book antidote to this idea. See for instance p. 30, where Smart presents considerations of great generality but also of importance in this connection. Bernard Williams' essay 'Tertullian's Paradox' is subtle yet lucid, careful yet bold. MacKinnon brings before our minds how easy it is to assume too soon that words which sound like nonsense are nonsense and how difficult it may be to come at what sense they have. But I will not attempt to mention each essay in this book. I would like to say something of its purpose and to try to make clearer a certain issue which is, I think, the most general, if not the main, issue which it presents. This issue is also a main issue

[1] *New Essays in Philosophical Theology.* Edited by Anthony Flew and Alasdair MacIntyre. (S.C.M. Press) 21s.

in Professor Braithwaite's Eddington lecture, *An Empiricist's View of the Nature of Religious Belief.*[2]

The title *Essays in Philosophical Theology* suggests philosophical arguments for or against the existence of God, or his omnipotence, or his goodness, or his having created the world, or his now controlling it, and that sort of thing. This idea may, before one opens the book, prompt one to ask, 'But how can philosophical arguments settle such questions as these? In general, how can philosophical argument be relevant to questions of fact? And surely the question "Is there a God or is there not?" is a question of fact, and surely the question "Is the world guided by God or isn't it?" is also a question as to what in fact is so?'

However, in spite of the title, the book does not take up such questions as 'Does God exist?', 'Does God influence or control Nature?' or any other theological question. What it is mainly concerned with is the general character of such questions. Are they questions of fact? And if so what sort of facts would support an affirmative answer and what sort of facts would support a negative answer? And if they are not questions of fact what sort of questions are they? Are they perhaps questions calling less for enquiry than for decision?

We all know, in ourselves, the person who too often when a question is asked replies, 'But what do you mean?' We have read or been told that one ought to define one's terms and we at times now behave as if we were under the impression that no-one is in a fit condition to get on with the answering of a question unless he can define the terms in which that question is put. On the other hand we also know that though questions as to the meaning of a question are usually superfluous they are sometimes useful. The simplest cases of this sort arise when, although one knows the general nature of the question someone is asking, one doesn't know whether he is using a certain expression, for instance 'cousin', in this sense or in that sense. Sometimes we may suspect that the speaker himself has not quite made up his mind about this. For instance, those who speak of 'a first cause' seem sometimes to waver between using

---

[2] *An Empiricist's View of the Nature of Religious Belief.* By R. B. Braithwaite. (Cambridge University Press) 3s. 6d.

this expression to mean no more than 'the cause which precedes all other causes' and using it to mean a great deal more than this. In addition to difficulties of this sort there do occasionally arise difficulties as to what one might call 'the general character' of a question. I mean when someone asks, 'Was it criminal?' one may reply, 'Are you asking a legal question or a moral question?' If someone asks, 'Ought we, perhaps, not to have declared war when Germany invaded Poland?' one may reply, 'Are you asking a moral question or a question as to what it would have been expedient to do?' What is more, it does occasionally, very occasionally, happen that a person asks a question about the general character of a very familiar sort of question, a sort of question the general character of which he, in a sense, already knows. For instance there have been people who, suddenly struck by the difference between questions as to what lies in the past and what lies in the lumber room, have found themselves asking, 'But are these questions about the past of a sort which can be answered by that search for old bones, stones, documents, photos in the family album, pictures in the memory, on which we must rely?' Others have replied, 'But surely questions about the past just *are* questions about what we shall find when we try to answer them?' or again there have been those who have asked, 'What is mind? Is it reducible to a pattern of behaviour?' There have been those who have asked, 'What is matter?' and then embarked, not on a scientific investigation, but on the meta-question 'Are questions about material things in the end questions as to what sensations we shall get when we try to answer them?'

These metaphysical enquiries, these questions as to the nature of some type of question, T, seldom much help or hinder those who are grappling with questions of that type, especially when T is a very familiar, everyday, type of question. Historians, for instance, have, so far as I know, been very little influenced, whether for good or ill, by the work of those metaphysical philosophers who have asked themselves the curious question, 'How is any question about the past to be settled?' Again, among the questions which very much concern us are questions as to whether a person has done well or badly in doing what he has done. There has been much discussion amongst metaphysical philosophers as to how, if at all, any of these questions are to be met. But has all this discussion made much difference to anyone grappling with one of these questions? The answer, I believe, is No.

Is this unfortunate? Would it be worth while for those who are concerned with questions of right and wrong to consider the method appropriate to them before embarking upon them? Would it be worth their while to consider how far such questions are questions of taste and how far they are not? Such a study of the nature of moral questions often leads to 'views' of the nature of moral questions. For instance it may lead to the 'view' that moral questions aren't really questions, that one who answers a moral question is simply saying, 'Do this sort of thing', or 'Don't do this sort of thing', or 'I myself aim to do (or not to do) this sort of thing' and is thus declaring a policy or recommending a policy. If we reply, 'But surely one who answers a moral question "Would it be right to do this now?" is different from one who declares or enjoins an agricultural policy and even from one who offers a counsel of expediency?' we may receive the answer, 'Of course he differs. He differs in the sort of considerations he offers in support of his policy. But this leaves untouched the truth that one who says, "It was wrong" is not making a statement which calls for efforts to come at its truth like the statement, "This man is solvent", or "This argument is valid", or "In Smith *v.* Baker there was not *consent to risk*".'

But is this right? Aren't we being led up the garden path? When someone now looks back on what has happened and asks, 'But *was* it all so right, so admirable?' isn't he wondering whether he hasn't been mistaken, blind? Doesn't he put all his mind with all his heart into trying to see things now, not as they then appeared, but more nearly as they were? Isn't he trying to reach the truth however long he has been lost, and may still be lost, in the infinite dialectic of good and evil?

It is not our business now to go further into the metaphysic of morals, into the attempt to portray one who is engaged on a question as to the better and the worse. We have seen enough to see that it isn't easy to do this, and that it is easy to offer as a portrait what is a caricature.

And the metaphysic of morals is no exception. Hasn't the metaphysical study of a family of questions again and again led to caricature, and caricature which is presented with all the air of not being a caricature? By dint of comparing rival accounts of the character of a class of questions, we may, by a dialectic process, come to see as we had not done before the character of those questions. But, even if we have some success in this, shall we deal with those questions any better than we did before?

In spite of all this the contributors to this book seem agreed that it is worth while for those who are concerned with questions and statements involving the existence of God to consider the appropriate way to meet these questions and statements. They do not mean, of course, that no-one should venture to say anything about God who has not first considered the mode of verification proper to his statement. They are aware that to know what would show a statement to be true or to be false is not to know that it is true. (In connection with this point: extreme circumspection is needed in reading what Professor Smart says on p. 41. He points out that in the case of some questions, such as 'Do electrons exist?' it is hardly possible to know properly their meaning without having had pointed out to one samples of the phenomena referred to by one who makes statements which imply an affirmative answer. This must not make us forget that even when the best way of explaining the meaning of a statement includes pointing to samples of what is referred to in such a statement, it remains true that to know what would need to be so if that statement were to be true, is not the same thing as knowing that what would need to be so is so.) Mr. Williams (p. 206) remarks that it is very difficult for anyone to describe the character of religious statements who has never felt much need to make them. One who has never felt and known the difference between a coloured photograph of a picture and the original is not well fitted to describe what we do when in this sphere we speak of what is small, great, trivial, excellent.

In spite of all this these writers embark on a study of the nature of religious belief; and, for myself, I am ready to agree that metaphysics is here not less dangerous but less superfluous than usual. For this there are two reasons.

(1) Our metaphysical innocence in this sphere is already lost. Things have already been said about the nature of religious

belief, and what has been said, while it may show us what we had not noticed, may also seriously mislead us. For instance there have been those who have given the impression that it is proper to accept statements about God without having reason to think them true or even without understanding them.

When someone speaks or writes in a way which gives this impression about anything which others say—whether it be what is said by poets or mystics or religious teachers or philosophers—one feels a need to understand what he means and to consider how far what *he* is saying is true.

For how *can* one believe what one does not understand? How *can* one properly believe what one has not reason to believe? I am not saying that there is nothing to be said in answer to these questions. Words may come into a man's mouth and he may then say that he doesn't know what he meant by them. Later he may say, 'Ah, now I see what I meant'. But all talk about 'believing what one doesn't understand' or 'having a right to believe what one has no reason to believe' needs careful explanation if one is to avoid 'all appearance of evil', the evil of saying what may seem to encourage confusion, superstition, and the determination of our beliefs by our desires.

Then, also, there have been those who have given the impression that, if those who make statements involving the existence of God are making statements of fact at all, then the question whether they are right must be one to be settled by experiments not yet carried out, by further experience; that otherwise 'God's in his heaven' means no more than the comment 'Nature is orderly' or 'life preserving' or something of that sort, or no more than the sort of thing meant *nowadays* by one who says, 'The moon has hid her face'—a dead metaphor and one which remarks only what everyone recognizes, and, beyond that, meaning nothing.

(2) A second reason for thinking that the metaphysics of religion may be of some small use to religion is this. Metaphysical pronouncements to the effect that for a certain class of statements no reasons are needed, or to the effect that any reasons for a certain class of statement must be of this sort or of that can often be safely ignored. Mathematicians do not need the philosophy of mathematics, and those who ask the times of

trains to Town do not need to bother about the philosophy of the external word. But then their enquiries are of types with which we are most thoroughly at home. Now statements about God, though we may have heard them at our mother's knee, are rather strange. The statement, 'You might think that there is no-one who guides the world and loves it, but there is—high above' has not quite the character it at first appears to have, unless it is to be interpreted on the lines 'You might think there is no-one here but you and me, but there is —behind the curtain.' But as children we were taught that the statement is not to be interpreted exactly on these lines—we were told that God is invisible. Electrons, of course, are not visible like bees, and yet after some initial bewilderment we come to regard statements about them with only a trace of anxiety. Again, we come to accept, or at least to understand, the strange and somewhat elusive statement that 'Energy is everywhere and eternal.' Even the strange statement 'You might think that life was driven by hate and an overweening wish for power, but really it is driven by a never satisfied longing for affection and loyalty' —even that hazy, elusive statement has not about it all those difficulties which we feel about the more familiar statement, 'It may not seem so at first glance, but God knows it all and loves us still'.

It is easy to recall in outline what it is that makes many people feel that they don't know what is meant by those who speak of God, and what it is that has driven some people to ask 'Do those who speak of God really assert anything as to what is so? Aren't their words mainly, primarily, the expression of their commitment to a way of life?' For those who have spoken of and still speak of God often do so without a trace of doubt although at first there seems little to support what they say and much against it. Asked the reason for what they assert they seem to point to nothing which isn't known to everyone, and— a different point—to nothing which justifies their confidence. They often speak of God's unfailing love and of his tremendous power, in spite of all the wretchedness in the world, the misery that is apparent and the misery that is hidden. Are they blind? Are they crazy? Of course, they do not deny that there have been famines, pestilences, wars. But after all, a man can admit all these and yet never really see, never realize what has gone on and does go on—until perhaps something happens which brings it home to him. I always remember how when I was a child I was told of a woman in our village who, after her son had been killed in the 1914 war, said that she could no longer believe in God. At the time I thought this an audacious inference. Perhaps it was. But one must not forget how a single incident may suddenly throw a light on ten thousand others which one had managed to forget or never seen for what they were. To that woman no doubt it seemed that those who spoke to her of God were blind like one who will not see, or like one who crazily insists that he is the Emperor of China, or that his relatives and the doctors are against him, aim to poison him—not at once, of course, that is why they feed him and even seem to exert themselves on his behalf. One who, as we say, suffers from such a delusion, almost forgives the naïveté with which we fail to detect the hidden malice, the secret evil in the world. Is he like those who regretfully accept our inability to recognize the magnificence and the good of the world that God has made?

But it would be unjust to pretend that all religious people will not or cannot recognize the distress and the evil in the world. On the contrary, those who speak of God and sin and the vanity of many things, often bring to mind more boldly than those who do not the distress of guilt and of disappointment with ourselves and with others. 'The whole creation', St. Paul says, 'groaneth and travaileth until now.' '. . . what I would', he says, 'that I do not; but what I hate that do I.' This is not denial, this is not evasion. In speaking as he does of the extent of pain and the power of evil St. Paul is not alone among religious teachers. In this at least religion reveals the truth. And it does so not by telling us what we did not know but by showing us what we did.

It is when religious people preach good news and tell us that all may yet be well, that their words seem to some to express a foolish confidence, a senselessly invulnerable optimism. St. Paul, for instance, insists that we are saved by hope, declares that as in Adam all die, so in Christ shall all be made alive, refers us to the resurrection of Jesus, of how he was seen by Cephas, then of the twelve, after that of above five hundred brethren at once. Again he is not alone in using words which seem directed towards showing us, not now hidden powers for evil, confusion and pain, but hidden powers for good, understanding and pleasure. There are few religions which offer no hope. They join in insisting that there is power which can save us if we will avail ourselves of it. No matter what happens, no matter what is learned of how the world came to be what it is, and of how it works, those who speak of God and a power for good from which we may turn, on which we may draw, speak still with undiminished confidence. It's their strange obstinacy, it's their confidence which seems so unamenable to reason, so insensitive to what is so, that puts into the mind the suggestion that their words express no claim as to what is or is not the case, that 'the primary use of religious assertions is to announce allegiance to a set of principles' and not to tell us what does or does not exist.

It is tempting at once to reject the suggestion that the primary use of religious assertions is to announce allegiance to a set of moral principles, without considering what it does and does not amount to. We must remember that one who makes this suggestion may admit that many of those who have spoken of God or the Devil have with their words expressed some claim as to matters of fact. He may even allow that *strictly speaking* a statement is not, in the ordinary usage of the word, religious, unless it includes a claim of fact. He may allow that it is paradoxical to say that a man believes in God only because he gives water to the thirsty and food to the hungry (Matt. xxv, 34) and yet insist that this paradox yields a new conception of religion which shows us 'the heart of the matter', emphasizes that in the meaning of religious statements which we most mean to mark when we distinguish them as *religious*.

'What is meant', you may ask, 'by talk about a certain feature, F, being in strictness necessary for a thing's being of a certain kind, K, and yet not a *primary* necessity for its being of that kind, K, or not of the *essence* of K?' A person who allows that strictly speaking a creature is not, in the ordinary usage of the word, a man unless he has two legs, no wings, and does not too strangely appear and disappear, may yet insist that the essence of a man lies in his spiritual nature and not in his lack of feathers, his form, or his steady obedience to the laws of physics. Such a person claims that whether or not having the form of a man is necessary to a creature's being a man it is not a *primary* necessity for a creature's being a man. Even if, speaking strictly in accordance with the usage of language to date, it were improper to speak of 'action at a distance' we might yet claim that to speak of action at a distance is not to take from the notion of action any *essential* feature. And it is *conceivable* that someone should remark this without there having occurred any phenomena in nature which call for this modified notion of action.

But is it true that it is no part of the essence of what we understand by the title 'a religious assertion' that that assertion should make a claim as to what is fact is so?

Consider first the following somewhat paradoxical account of the mythology, or, if you like, the theology, of the Greeks. Imagine that someone says: 'When the Greeks spoke of their gods, of the power of Aphrodite and the need to remember Dionysus, what they really meant was something which life in instance after instance confirms. Nor does the fact that the phenomena they referred to are experienced in some measure by us all imply that their theology tells no-one anything he does not already know. For we may be extremely familiar with phenomena of a certain sort, for instance gravitational phenomena, and yet be quite unable or unwilling to put two and two together until someone finds words for it all and with them shows us the connections in what seemed unconnected, obliges us to recognize what is for what it is. I myself do not expect my sheep to do badly if I do not make sacrifices to Apollo, nor do I sometimes half fear to see, under the shadow of the trees, Cypris herself. Nevertheless, I believe so much of what the Greeks expressed in their stories of the gods that I count myself as one who holds beliefs not different in essentials from theirs'.

All this makes little of differences between two set of beliefs, differences so considerable that one may hesitate to agree that they are 'not essential'. However the demythologized beliefs were latent in the old beliefs, and at least the new beliefs are still beliefs as to what in fact is so. Because of these affinities in content and in general character it is perhaps not too misleading to say that the two systems of beliefs are 'not essentially

different'. Or, if this seems to be going too far, we may say
perhaps that both systems of beliefs are 'in essence religious'.
Some people after all might say that the words used by the old
geometers, when they first began to set out the properties of
triangles, parallel lines and the rest, expressed beliefs not essentially different from those set out with the same words by a
modern geometer, even if the modern geometer is setting out
only the implications of concepts and is asserting nothing
as to what is so in nature, while the old geometers half intended
their statements as descriptions of nature. And we may at least
allow that both systems of beliefs or assertions were in essence
geometrical, and that it is not of the essence of a geometrical
assertion that it should say anything about what nature is
like. Even if we insist (1) that beliefs or assertions which imply
nothing which could conceivably have been false are essentially
different from beliefs or assertions which do imply something as to what only happens to be so, we may yet allow (2)
that both the assertions of the early geometers and the assertions of a pure geometer are in essence geometrical assertions.
We may say that it is not of the essence of geometry that it
should include assertions which could conceivably have been
false, assertions as to what the world is actually like.

But now consider someone who says that when he speaks
of the gods he uses the old words not to say anything as to what
the world is like nor anything of which one might ask 'Is it
true?', but only to express his commitment to a way of life
which, come what may, he will pursue. And suppose that this
really is all that he means to do when he speaks of the gods.

Then, when he speaks of the gods, his words are not meaningless. Far from it. Those who at Colenso in response to the appeal
'Volunteers for the guns' put up their hands, quoted no odds
on any event. But they meant what they said. As none could
deny who then saw them take their teams through a hail of
bullets to bring in those guns.

Nevertheless we must insist that a person who in speaking
of the gods expresses no belief as to what in fact is so is essentially different from one who does. Can we allow that his words
still express what are in essence religious beliefs? Can we say
that it is not of the essence of what we mean by a religious

pronouncement that it should express some belief as to what the world is like?

I cannot here argue this question at length. But I believe the answer is No. It seems to me that some belief as to what the world is like is of the essence of religion.

Compare a case in which someone says that though one might naturally think that a search for the truth is of the essence of what is done in a court of law, this is a mistake. 'Those questions', he says, 'which lawyers argue even when everyone knows what has happened, are not really questions. They are calls for a decision on a word and, with the word, on what shall be done; a decision which shall be morally right or socially expedient'.

To this philosopher of the law I should feel bound to reply: But this is false. Lawyers, like the rest of us, may sometimes yield to the temptation to distort the truth for purposes good or bad. But when lawyers argue before a court such a question as, 'Was there negligence or was there not?' 'Was there consent to risk or was there not?', then those lawyers and that court, subject to human frailty, aim at the truth. Such questions, it is true, may be argued when 'we all know what happened' as well as one knows what happened when one asks of one's own action 'Was it cruel?' 'Was it mean?' On such occasions no further observation, no experiment will settle the matter. But 'Was there negligence or was there not?' is no less a question as to what is or was so than is the question 'Is this firm solvent or is it not?' which an accountant may ask *even when he has before him all the information he needs*. An accountant, it is true, may often, by a definite step-by-step procedure, reach a definite answer which fairly enough presents the situation he aims to grasp. Such a procedure, and even such an answer, is often impossible for a court of law. But whether or not the truth a court seeks can be presented in an answer 'Yes' or 'No', the question it asks and the procedure it adopts is directed towards a firmer, fairer apprehension of what it was that happened.

Perhaps the philosopher replies: 'It's true, no doubt, that lawyers and courts of law in fact in the course of their proceedings often bring out the truth. But this is a means to an end—justice or the welfare of the people. A person who wishes to induce you to act rightly may and often does point out fact and circumstance. But what we call moral reasoning is in essence a procedure for inducing a certain attitude and a course of action. And what we call legal reasoning is in essence a publicly recognized form of procedure for inducing authorities to adopt a certain attitude and, especially, to take certain action.' But this won't do. It is of the essence of the law, not merely that justice be done, but that it be seen to be done. Neither legal enquiry nor moral enquiry is or could be a process in which, by hook or by crook, we induce an attitude and promote a policy. Argument must be heard. Argument which is not merely any psychological procedure which obtains a certain result, but a procedure in which we set this by that, and that by this, so as to see more plainly than we did at first what it was that happened, and then and only then to act. To describe such a procedure as a process primarily of persuasion to a line of action, to say that a search for the truth is not of the essence of this procedure, is to say what is dangerous, defamatory and false.

Those who have suggested that it is not of the essence of religion to say something as to what in fact is so have spoken no doubt with the best intentions. In any case this is not itself a religious statement but only a piece of philosophy about religious statements. Even so it will be understandable if one to whom his religion means much calls this piece of philosophy 'a blasphemous fable and a dangerous deceit'. For it tries to take from the doctrines of religion, not merely something without which they would not *strictly* speaking be religious, but something without which they would no longer be themselves.

When St. Paul said 'The wages of sin is death' he said what, though it is not obviously true, is yet something which, to say the least, may be true. It involved moral judgement and it involved also an assertion as to what happens. When Jesus said 'Except a man be born again he cannot see the kingdom of God' (John iii, 3), Nicodemus replied 'How can a man be born when he is old?' Jesus did not, in response, explain that he had meant nothing as to what in fact is so. On the contrary, he said 'We speak that we do know and testify that we have seen'. The words 'If ye forgive not men their trespasses, neither will your

E

Father forgive your trespasses' (Matt. vi, 15) seem to convey a warning. The words 'If ye forgive men their trespasses your heavenly Father will also forgive you' seem to convey a hope. Whether or not the hope is false or unfounded it was hope they were intended to convey. And the words 'In my Father's house are many mansions, if it were not so, I would have told you' say something as to what is so.

Words which do not do this are, *ipso facto*, profoundly different. And they will lack, so I submit, what is of the essence of religion.

VI

The Metamorphosis of Metaphysics

I speak of the metamorphosis of metaphysics because I want to trace a change in identity and an identity in change in the development of metaphysics. People sometimes speak as if the metaphysician were a pretentious and really very silly old man who is now dead, and has been replaced first by the logical analyst, and later by someone still more on the spot, the linguistic philosopher. It seems to me misleading to talk like this. True, when someone whom we know very well changes very profoundly we may say, 'He is no longer the same person.' And saying this we combat the deadly inertia of our minds which makes us dismiss as a mere pretence anything in what a man says or does which does not fit the picture of him which the past has given us. Jack, who never misses a party and 'always has some new crack', is suddenly serious and insists that he would like to throw it all up and grow roses. Even if we do not say 'Nonsense', we still cannot help a smile which shows him that we do not take seriously what he is saying. It's this inertia in our awareness of each other which is one of the things which often makes a person unable to talk to someone who knows him well in the way he can to a stranger. For a stranger will not laugh when he says what is out of character, or rather, what does not fit the model of him which the past has presented to others and even to himself. But, on the other hand, a stranger may be misled if he takes present appearance as the sole clue to a person's real nature. The last phase of a man's life may show us something in him which never appeared in his youth, but it may also conceal from us something which once showed plain enough though now it never shows except in some flicker of word or manner, significant only to one who knew him long ago. He has now, perhaps, sat for years at a window gazing at a landscape in suburbia. This too, it is true, shows his nature. But the secret of this inanition may elude us until we learn of something that went before, never forgotten but never recalled.

All this reminds us of the laborious, intricate, subtle process by which, alive to the variety in perpetual change, we yet in that variety detect a unity, in the obvious the hidden, in appearance reality. It is something we never cease from doing, whether in everyday life, in poetry, in drama, in history, in science, in philosophy, and even in metaphysical philosophy which also, so it has been commonly said, is somehow concerned with appearance and reality.

So in the hope of gaining a better grasp of the real nature of metaphysical philosophy or, as one might call it, the philosophy of the schools, let us look back at how it once appeared and at what came after. And in doing this let us look at three things: first at what metaphysical philosophers said about philosophy; second, at how they formulated metaphysical questions; third, at what they did in order to answer these questions.

About 1920 Dr. J. Ellis McTaggart was still lecturing at Cambridge and he might be called the last of the 'speculative' philosophers at Cambridge or even in England. Although he knew Russell and Moore he still put metaphysical philosophical questions in the traditional forms 'Is time real?' 'Does matter exist?' 'Philosophy,' he used to say, 'is the systematic study of the ultimate nature of reality.' The scientist, he said, studies systematically the nature of reality but not its ultimate nature. The poet, he said, does not study the nature of reality systematically, but he does study its ultimate nature. This last remark is an important clue to what he meant by the mysterious phrase 'the ultimate nature of reality'. For it appears that this phrase refers to something which at least some poets do which scientists do not do or do much less. But what is this? Which poets do it and when do they do it most? So far as I know, McTaggart said little or nothing in further explanation of this reference to poetry. Why not? What did he mean? What made him say that poets study the ultimate nature of reality? On the face of it it would seem that a metaphysical philosopher is much more like a scientist than he is like a poet, and surely the scientist does in some sense study the ultimate

nature of matter and even of mind. One would not be surprised
to hear a scientist say that it has been discovered that objects
which seem to us solid are not really solid, that our flesh and
bones, and chairs and tables, and even stones, are ultimately
not solid, that ordinary experience makes us think they are
solid but extraordinary experience enables us, if not to observe
at least to infer that they are not. All this reminds us at once
of metaphysical philosophers who have said that though things
seem large and round and soft or hard, small and angular,
they are not; that though they seem to come and go they do
not; that though they seem to be in space and time they are not.
It reminds us of philosophers who have said that what seems to
us physical and material is not, that our bodies and even chairs
and tables and stones are not material but are really collections
of ideas, impressions, sensations, in our minds, or in the mind
of some timeless being. The metaphysical philosopher seems
for a moment to differ from the scientist only in that he goes
further. The editor of *Contemporary British Philosophy* at the end
of the preface to the second volume of this collection of philosophers' writings speaks of their common purpose of 'exploring
the frontier provinces of human experience and perchance
bringing back authentic tidings of what lies beyond'. But now is
it characteristic of the philosopher to explore the frontier provinces of human experience? Is it not much less Aristotle,
Descartes, Hume, Kant, and much more Flaubert, Dostoevsky,
Kafka, Lawrence, Freud, who 'travel to the bounds of human
experience'? And do these explorers attempt to bring back
tidings of anything that lies beyond human experience? Surely
it is with human experience itself that they are concerned. What
they write about may be as imaginary as the frictionless planes
and perfect pulleys of the engineer, but this leaves it true that
what they are concerned with in the end is the wide but well-
known world.

But we must leave this matter for the moment and ask what
questions McTaggart and the traditional metaphysical philosophers asked themselves. They asked, 'Is time real?' 'Does
matter exist?' 'Does mind exist?' 'Does evil exist?' 'These
things', they said, 'appear to be real but are they? After all
what seems to be so is sometimes shown by further experience
to be an illusion. Perhaps what all experience *superficially*

suggests is so, more fundamental thought may show to be an illusion too, to be appearance and not ultimately real.'

These are traditional questions in their traditional form.

What a change then, what a shocking change, came over the scene when in 1918 Moore wrote, 'The questions whether we do ever know such things as these, and whether there are any material things seem to me, therefore, to be questions which there is no need to take seriously: they are questions which it is quite easy to answer, with certainty, in the affirmative.'[1] What a change when Moore, in lecturing on the soul, the self, the mind, the ego, declared that he would not concern himself with the question 'Does the soul exist?' but with the question 'What do we mean when we say such things as "I see this", "I did see that" '. What a change when in 1914 Russell said that he believed that the problems and the method of philosophy had been misconceived by all schools,[2] that philosophical problems all reduce themselves, in so far as they are genuinely philosophical, to problems of logic.[3] For instance, the traditional philosophers had troubled themselves with the question 'How can such beings as Zeus, the horses of the gods, and Mr. Pecksniff, not have being, not exist? For how can what does not exist be thought of or talked of, how can it entertain or annoy us? How can what does not exist have any property?' Russell showed that this old riddle vanishes under logical analysis as surely as does the riddle 'What happens when an irresistible force meets an immovable object?' He then turned his attention to those philosophers who prove, not that things which do not exist do, but that things which do exist do not, or at least that there is no real reason to think they do. For instance, McTaggart[4] at the end of a discussion as to the existence of matter concludes that there is no more reason to think that the causes of our sensations are coloured, warm, large, round, or heavy than there is to think that the face of one who boils a lobster red must itself be red. He says, 'The result is that matter is in the same position as the Gorgons or the Harpies. Its existence is a bare

---

[1] Quoted by Professor Morris Lazerowitz in 'Moore's Paradox' in *The Philosophy of G. E. Moore*.

[2] *Our Knowledge of the External World*, p. 3.

[3] Ibid., p. 33.

[4] *Some Dogmas of Religion*, section 73.

possibility to which it would be foolish to attach the least importance since there is nothing to make it at all preferable to any other hypothesis however wild.' Other philosophers felt that this was going rather far. And Russell, remembering the sophistical performance in which philosophers had made it appear that Gorgons and Harpies do exist, now ventured a suggestion to those who were purporting to prove that chairs and tables do not exist.

> Look here, [he said],[1] surely what you really mean is not that chairs and tables are fictions like the Gorgons and the Harpies, but that they are *logical* fictions like force or the economic man or the average Englishman. You do not really mean that everyone who says anything about chairs and tables is hopelessly mistaken or irrational. What you mean is that just as the statements about the average Englishman can be analysed without remainder into statements about individual Englishmen whom we see everyday, so statements about chairs and tables can be analysed without remainder into statements about what we can expect to see and feel.

There was something attractive about this suggestion. But it was revolutionary. It was not that no one had suggested before that to speak of material things is to speak of bundles of impressions or sensations. What was so unpleasantly revolutionary was the suggestion that metaphysical philosophers who had seemed to be concerned not with any merely logical question but with whether matter exists were really concerned with a logical question. Philosophers of the old school stood aghast yet unable to check the rapid metamorphosis of a subject which had been a study of the nature of reality and now seemed no more than the purely logical investigation of the structure of propositions, the minute analysis of the meanings of words. But we who were the bright young things of the logico-analytic era welcomed the change from the absurdity of exploring the universe in an armchair to the pleasure of a dance beneath the brilliant lights of *Principia Mathematica*. We even joined hands in a party with the pragmatists amid the ruins of tradition.[2]

---

[1] See, for instance, *Our Knowledge of the External World*, especially Lecture III.

[2] Here remember James's camping party and what he calls a metaphysical dispute about a squirrel: *Pragmatism*, Lecture II.

Even after the revolution certain difficulties beset us. Logical fictions, logical constructions, seemed to be everywhere. We did not mind that. But exactly how were they constructed and out of what? Chairs and tables, Russell had taught us, were no 'part of the ultimate furniture of heaven and earth'. But on what then could we rest? Sense data perhaps, the constituents of the ultimate atomic facts corresponding to the atomic propositions into which all other propositions can be analysed. But now what is it to analyse a proposition? It is to analyse the meaning of a sentence. But then what is the meaning of a sentence and what is it to analyse it? However to this we soon had an answer. To analyse a class of propositions, we said, is to translate a class of sentences. For instance, to analyse propositions about material things into propositions about sense data or sensations is to translate sentences about chairs and tables into sentences about sense data or sensations, to analyse propositions about good and evil into propositions about our feelings is to translate sentences of the sort 'This is good', 'That is bad', into sentences of the sort 'I like this' or 'We disapprove that'.

With this advance we did not *deny* that philosophy is a matter of the logical analysis of propositions, but we *supplemented* this account of philosophy with the explanation 'And the analysis of propositions is the translation of sentences.' This advance has sometimes been referred to as a change from 'the material mode of speech' to 'the formal mode'. It is the change from a mode of speech in which a speaker appears to refer to a logical, abstract entity, such as a proposition, into a mode of speech in which he apparently refers to a word or a sentence.

Although this change from the logical to the linguistic mode of formulating philosophical questions was not adopted by all philosophers of the logico-analytic group one must not forget its importance. For with it went a change in what philosophers did in answering philosophical questions. While one speaks of 'analysing propositions' one speaks of 'trying to see their structure', 'trying to see whether one thing is or is not part of another'. When one speaks of translating sentences one speaks of inquiring into a plain matter of fact, namely whether people would or would not always be prepared to substitute a certain expression for another.

This change was indeed important. It cleared away, or

seemed to clear away, or in part cleared away, the exasperating hesitancy one felt as to what to do when philosophers disagreed as they sometimes still did even after the logico-analytic reformation. An appeal to the self-evident, to the intuitively obvious, leads sometimes to unpleasant hints of blindness or of seeing what is not there. What a relief to turn instead to the plain facts of linguistic usage! But this change must not be thought of as a change from a logical phase in which one asked *only* questions as to the interrelations between such timeless entities as propositions and predicates, and *never* asked 'What would we say?' to a linguistic phase in which one asked *only* 'What would we say?' No, the change was not so sharp as this. In the logical phase questions were put in the form 'What is the analysis of propositions of the sort so and so?' But no one who remembers, for instance, Moore's lectures of that time will forget the frequent appeals to what one would in ordinary language say. The change was more like this: In the logical phase we thought of recalling the usage of words as a *means* to insight into the structure of the abstract entities, the propositions and the properties for which those words stood. In the linguistic phase the usage of words appears to be itself the ultimate object of study. Imagine someone concerned with the relations between blocks made of ice or glass so transparent as to be almost invisible. He may sometimes find it difficult to answer a question as to whether one block does or does not extend beyond another. But if each block is enclosed in a coloured frame which in most cases fits it pretty well then he may as a first step answer questions about the relations between the frames and so reach indirectly answers to questions about the relations between the blocks. How much more boldly though, how much more freely, will he give his attention to the frames if we tell him that we are no longer interested in their contents, if they have any contents at all. In the same way, or so it seemed, when we describe philosophy no longer as the physics of the abstract to which the usage of words may provide useful clues but as itself the study of the usage of words then we are freed from trying to see those meanings which seem to grow more hazy as we gaze at them and may turn with relief to a task anyone who is patient can do, namely that of recalling the usage of words.

And this advance to the boldly, not to say blatantly, linguistic phase led to another important change. It showed a way out from an impasse produced by an obsession with definition and exact equivalence. Russell before our fascinated gaze had, as I have said, despatched the inhabitants of the world of fiction and of legend, such as unicorns and the ram which flew or swam from Greece to Colchis, those bewildering beings which have never existed and yet, it seems, must linger somewhere in the realms of being, if they are to be so much as the subjects of a conversation. He had despatched them by providing a rule for analysing the propositions which seem to be about such beings into equivalent propositions which no longer seem to be about such beings because they are plainly only about descriptions of these beings. It was no wonder that, slightly inebriated by this success, we supposed that the same procedure must be at once sufficient and necessary to dissipate such philosophical disputes as those about the existence of material things, or of mental things.

Alas the exact analyses were not forthcoming, or rather at one moment it seemed as if they were and at the next as if they were not. Russell would suggest in the *Analysis of Matter* or the *Analysis of Mind* the lines on which with a little care the requisite analyses could be found. But Moore would produce some objection to the correctness of the suggested equations.

While philosophical problems were put in the form 'What are the propositions which together make up the ultimate parts of what we mean when we speak of things of sort X?' it seemed essential to find parts which made up exactly that of which they formed the parts. And when the philosophical problems were recast in the linguistic mode 'Can sentences of sort X be translated into sentences not of sort X?' it seemed essential to find sentences not of sort X which meant neither more nor less than sentences of sort X. But these translations could not be found. And this was not because of an accidental paucity of the English, French, or German language. It was no accident at all. The most typical tough old metaphysical puzzles are just those which arise when, pressing a question of the form 'What ultimately are our reasons for statements of sort X?', we come at last to reasons which though they are all we have are *not* such that statements of sort X can be deduced from them whether singly or in combination. The difficulty would be removed if we could say that statements of sort X are reducible to those upon the truth of which our confidence in statements of sort X is ultimately based. But the difficulty is that statements of sort X are not deducible from those on which they are ultimately based and therefore not reducible to them, not analysable into them; in other words a typical metaphysical difficulty about what is expressed by sentences of sort X cannot be met by translating those sentences into others. Remember the pattern of metaphysical trouble. For instance, someone says, 'Has anything happened before this moment? Has there been a past? Do we know what we claim to know about the past?' You are amazed at such a crazy question. However, you reply perhaps, 'Well I know I wound my watch this morning.' But the sceptic asks, 'How do you know you did?' You are again amazed but still you perhaps reply, 'I always wind it when I get up and I certainly got up this morning.' The sceptic replies, 'If you knew these two statements to be true you could indeed deduce that you wound your watch this morning. But both these statements are statements about the past and are therefore included in those about which I am asking how you know them to be true.' You reply perhaps, 'I remember getting up this morning and for that matter I remember winding my watch.' The sceptic says, 'When you say that someone remembers an incident do you not imply that that incident took place?' You reply, 'Certainly. I could not remember winding my watch this morning if I did not wind it.' The sceptic says, 'So your claim to remember winding your watch this morning includes the claim that you wound it. It therefore includes a claim about the past. And I am therefore asking how you know that you do not merely seem to remember but do remember winding your watch this morning.' You reply, 'Well I certainly seem to remember winding it. I can see now a mental picture of the watch in my hand as I wind it. I do not need to know the past in order to know that I now see this mental picture. Besides here is the watch ticking away. If you now take a watch that is not going you will find that it will not go unless someone winds it and if you ask people whether they wound my watch this morning you will find that they all reply that they did not.' The sceptic says, 'But you can not deduce from all this about the present and the future that you wound your watch this morning nor anything else about the past.'

The position is becoming clear. Any statement from which a statement about the past can be deduced is or includes a statement about the past. And therefore to reduce the latter to the former is not to translate a sentence about the past into one which is not about the past. Any statement which is not about the past and does not openly or covertly include one, is not a statement from which a statement about the past can be deduced, and therefore not one to which a statement about the past can be reduced, and therefore the sentence which expresses it is not one into which a sentence about the past can be translated.

The position is the same for any typical metaphysical question.

How then, it may be asked, did it come about that Russell did meet a metaphysical difficulty by means of an analysis, a translation? The answer is that difficulty about how a classical scholar's statement such as 'The ram swam' can be true although there was no such ram is in an important respect like typical metaphysical difficulties but is also in an important respect unlike them. Suppose someone says: 'If a man marries the daughter of a daughter of his father's parents then he marries his cousin.' For a moment you may feel it difficult to be sure whether this is true or false. However you soon say, 'Well now this just means that if a man marries the daughter of a paternal aunt then he marries his cousin, and that of course is true.' Here reformulation has helped. But then the difficulty was not at all metaphysical.

Suppose now that a classical scholar says, 'The ram swam', and suppose that though usually you are quite sensible and well able to make sure whether such statements are right or wrong, you now suddenly feel a difficulty and say in a puzzled way, 'Surely this could be true although there was no such ram and yet how could it be?' This difficulty hardly hinders you in your grasp of the actual world as does a failure to realize that seven half-crowns is the right change from a pound when you have bought a two-and-sixpenny cake. The difficulty is like a metaphysical difficulty in that the question 'Surely this statement can be true and yet it cannot be' evinces at the same time an increased apprehension of the logical character of the statement and a misapprehension of its character. When suddenly one puts this question to oneself one is noticing more explicitly than one had done before a difference between the scholar's statement 'The ram swam' and the farmer's statement 'The ram swam.' At the same time this first expression of sharper apprehension is confused. It evinces a failure to see the peculiarity of the statement for what it is—an unusual, temporary, failure to keep its logical character firmly in mind.

On the other hand your question 'How can all these statements about what does not exist be true?' is not expressing mixed apprehension and misapprehension which extends to *all* statements equivalent to those you refer to. In your case there are statements equivalent to those you refer to about which you are not bewildered. Consequently your bewilderment can be removed by reminding you of this equivalence, by reformulating the statements which trouble you in statements which do not, by translating the sentences which temporarily mislead you as to the verification appropriate to what is asserted by those who utter them into sentences which make this plain, and, in particular, make plain how it is that what is expressed by them may be true although they are about things which do not exist.[1]

With a typical metaphysical statement or question the situation is different. Here the mixed apprehension and misapprehension extends to *all* statements equivalent to any member of the class of statements to which the metaphysician refers. In his case there are no statements which both (1) are equivalent to those to which he refers and (2) do not bewilder him. Consequently no translation will bring out and disentangle his apprehension and his misapprehension, no translation will transform his bewilderment into insight without distortion.

Does this mean that nothing can be done for the metaphysician because he is absurdly asking that statements exposed to certain risks of error shall be shown to be inevitable consequences of, deducible from, reformulatable in terms of, statements not exposed to those risks? It does not. It means that that is not what the metaphysician is asking for. Does this mean that the unsuccessful attempt to reformulate the metaphysician's question

[1] See W. E. Johnson, *Logic I*, p. 166.

"Beauty is Truth"

in the form 'Can sentences of sort X be translated into sentences of sort Y and not of sort X?' in no way helped us to understand what the metaphysician does ask for? It does not. On the contrary the question 'How can we translate sentences of sort X?' suggests the question 'How may we define sentences of sort X?' and this suggests the question 'How do we define the expression "is a sentence of sort X"?' and this suggests the question 'How shall we define the expression "is using a sentence of sort X" or "is using a sentence in the way X"?' And this suggests the questions 'How shall we explain, *whether by definition or not*, what it is to use a sentence in the way X?' 'How shall we describe a man who is using a sentence in the way X?'

There is a double change here. First there is a change from asking for a rule for translating sentences of sort X, for instance sentences about abstractions, such as the average man, the Indian elephant, to asking for a rule for translating sentences of the sort 'A is using a sentence of sort X', for instance, 'A is using a sentence about an abstraction.' This change is of importance because although any rule for translating sentences of sort X provides a rule for translating sentences of the sort 'A is using a sentence of sort X', the converse is not true. For instance, it is absurd to ask for a rule for translating sentences which attribute a property or relation to something into sentences which do not. But this does not mean that it is absurd to ask for a rule translating sentences of the sort 'A is using a sentence which attributes a property or relation to something.' The definition '*A is attributing a property*' means '*A is marking an affinity between something and other things real or imaginary*' is not far wrong.

The second change is a change from asking for a definition to asking for a description. We ask now *not for a definition* of what it is to use an expression, for instance, the word 'cold', to put a question as to the external world as opposed to a question as to how someone feels, but for some *explanation*, some *description*, of the differences between one who uses the expression to ask about the weather and one who uses it to ask someone how he feels.

This change too is important. Often when someone asks 'What is a so and so?' it is impossible to answer with a definition and often even when this is possible it is useless. Faced with this situation people sometimes say, 'We do not really know what it is for a thing to be a so and so' or, more moderately,

'We cannot say what it is, cannot put into words what it is, for a thing to be a so and so.' But this is because without knowing it they have become wedded to the idea that one does not know what it is for a thing to be of a certain sort unless one can give a definition of what it is to be of that sort, or to the more moderate but still false idea that one cannot put into words, explain, bring before the mind, what it is to be a thing of a certain sort except by a definition. The moment these ideas are formulated and so brought under the light of reason they disappear. Of course we know that the meanings of words are not taught only by definition in terms of other words, that is an absurd idea. And no doubt just as sometimes the meaning of a word is taught, introduced to the mind, not by definition but by examples real or imaginary and painted or described, so its meaning may be revived before the mind sometimes by definition but also sometimes by examples. But though the ideas that we do not know or cannot say what it is for a thing to be of a certain sort unless we can define it are rejected when plainly stated, they may continue to lurk in the mind. In order to *realize* their falsity as opposed to merely *knowing that* they are false let us look at one or two examples in which definition is impossible or futile while explanation by description and sample is possible and valuable. When someone asks, 'What is schizophrenia?' one may reply, 'A schizophrenic person is a person with a split mind.' This answer *may* satisfy the inquirer. But it may not. He may ask, 'But what is it to suffer from a split mind?' One may perhaps provide a definition of this expression too, but one may instead immediately employ what one may call 'mother's method' for explaining what things are. A child asks, 'What is a greyhound?' His father replies, 'A greyhound is a dog of a certain sort.' 'I know', says the child, 'but what sort?' 'Well', his father says, 'a greyhound is a dog in which the power to weight ratio. . . .' But his mother interrupts. 'Look', she says, 'that's a greyhound, and you remember your uncle's dog, Entry Badge, well that was a greyhound. But now that', she says, pointing to a Borzoi, 'is not a greyhound, and even that,' she says, pointing to a whippet, 'is not.' Or perhaps she recalls the rhyme

> A foot like a cat, a tail like a rat,
> A back like a rake, a head like a snake

and so on. In short the mother replies with instances of what is and what is not a greyhound or by comparing greyhounds with what they are not, and these two procedures merge into one. Asked 'What is the feminine nature?' we may reply with a definition, 'It is the nature of a female human being.' But somehow what we wanted is not contained in this easy and correct answer. Shakespeare takes longer to reply with his long stories of Juliet, of Desdemona, of Cressida, of Lady Macbeth, of Portia, of Orlando. And yet of course, his longer, less neat answer may show us as we had not yet seen it the unity in infinite variety which is the feminine nature, or, for that matter, human nature.

All this reminds us of how an answer to a 'What is a so and so?' question may be none the worse because it is not a definition, and may indeed be the better, because, more explicitly than any definition, it compares things of the sort with which we are concerned with other things, things which, though like, are different.

Remembering this we are no longer under a compulsion to provide a definition when someone asks, 'What is a poet?' 'What is a mathematician?' 'What is it to make a statement about mental things, about material things?' We are free to answer the questions 'Does matter exist?' 'What is matter?' not in the form of a definition of statements about material things but in the form of an account of what it is to make a statement about a material thing such as 'It's cold' or 'There are bees in that hive' as opposed to statements about things in the mind such as 'There are bees in his bonnet', or 'I am cold', or 'He has a warm heart.' And this account need not take the form of a definition provided it brings out by hook or by crook the unity within variety among statements about material things.

How satisfactory to pass from a phase in which philosophical questions seemed to call on us to explore some country we could never reach, to see behind some veil we could never penetrate, to open some door we could never open, to a phase in which no such demand is made of us but, instead, only the demand that we should analyse a class of propositions we often assert, translate a class of sentences we often utter. And then when it seems that we are being asked to translate the untranslatable, how satisfactory it is to find that this too is not being insisted upon, that we are being asked only to bring before the mind, by hook or by crook, the role these sentences perform, the procedure appropriate to ascertaining whether one who has pronounced such a sentence has spoken the truth or not, the logical character of a type of inquiry. For such a task though difficult and laborious is not impossible.

But now, just when all seems well, something seems to have been lost, and not merely something but too much. While we put our questions in the traditional form they were indeed intractable, but at least we seemed to be engaged on some task which somehow contributed to our apprehension of reality, of the facts, and this did not mean merely facts about how people would use words. Was this all a mistake?

Let us look back and I think we shall find that the first philosophical phase, properly understood, was not so unlike the last and then that the last, properly understood, is not so unlike the first.

Although the traditional philosophers described philosophy so differently, and formulated their questions so differently, did they proceed so differently from the way philosophers proceeded later? Take their attempts to show that matter does not exist. These attempts were of two sorts. There were attempts to show that matter, involving as it does time and space, involves a contradiction. Now one cannot prove statements self-contradictory except by a purely logical procedure; statements as to what is so though it might not have been and statements as to what is not so though it might have been, are beside the point. Consequently those philosophers who argued on these lines that there are no material things no more proceeded in a matter of fact manner than does one who proves that there are no equilateral triangles with unequal angles. Second, there were those philosophers who in considering the question 'Does matter exist?' proceeded as, for instance, McTaggart did in *Some Dogmas of Religion*. What does he say? He says (section 66), 'What reason can be given for a belief in the existence of matter? I conceive that such a belief can only be defended on the ground that it is a legitimate inference from our sensations,' 'It is evident', he says (section 68), 'that the sensations are not themselves the matter in question.' And as to the causes of the sensations, he says there is no reason to believe that they resemble the sensations in such a way that they, the causes, are entitled to the name of matter. At the end of section 73 he says,

> A man who boils a lobster red may have a red face—there is nothing to prevent it. But his action in causing the redness of the lobster gives us no reason to suppose that his face is red.
>
> The result is that matter is the same position as the Gorgons or the Harpies. . . .

At first it may appear that McTaggart is saying that though it is conceivable that we should have had reason to believe in the existence of matter we in fact have not. But careful examination of his argument reveals that at no point does it depend upon a statement which could have been false. His conclusion that we have no reason for our statements about material things is derived from the premiss (1) that if we have then those statements are legitimate inferences from our sensations and (2) that they are not legitimate inferences from our sensations— they are not legitimate *inductive* inferences, like conclusions as to what is behind one based on reflection in a mirror, nor are they legitimate *deductive* inferences, like conclusions as to the existence and nature of the honey bee based on premisses about honey bees.

If at this point someone were to say that McTaggart is really concerned with a question of logic, one might agree on the ground that though he makes some show of being concerned with something which might have been otherwise he is not. One might agree further that he is concerned with whether statements about material things are deducible from statements about our sensations. One could not agree that McTaggart is saying that statements about material things are reducible to statements about our sensations since he insists that the existence of matter is not deducible from such statements. On the other hand one might hesitate to say that he denies that statements about material things are reducible to statements about sensations. For in section 62 he says it is certain that my body influences myself, and in section 63 he says that I cannot change into bread the stone I see and touch, and in section 74 he says,

If we ask then of what reality the vast mass of knowledge holds true which science and everyday life give us about matter, we must reply that it holds true of various sensations which occur to various men, and of the law according to which these sensations are connected, so that from the presence of certain sensations in me I can infer that, under certain conditions, I shall or shall not experience certain other sensations and can also infer that, under certain conditions, other men will or will not experience certain sensations.

The fact is McTaggart, like Russell and others, is not sure which of two pictures of our knowledge of the material world he wishes to present. According to the first picture we are like prisoners confined in separate cells and never allowed to look out of the windows of their cells at the outside world nor to hear any sound of it. Each has a mirror, sound reflector, and other instruments which he believes reproduce faithfully what goes on outside his cell including what is reflected in the instruments of other prisoners. When a prisoner says something about the outside world, perhaps that the sun is shining, he does not mean merely that his instruments show the sun as shining nor even that his instruments and those of the other prisoners show the sun as shining. Not at all. He can remember other days, when he relied upon no mirrors or radio sets, and were he now given his freedom he would discard them all and say, 'The sun is shining' or 'The sun is not shining' no matter what might be the programme on the apparatus on which he is now obliged to rely. Indeed it is because when he speaks of the sun and the outside world he refers to something beyond what he can observe, the reflections in his instruments, that we must say that his knowledge of the outside world is indirect and not what it might be. According to McTaggart's first picture our knowledge of the material world is like the prisoner's knowledge of the world outside his cell, except that we are even worse off in that we have never known better days when we could turn from the shadow show of our sensations to the reality they reflect, nor can we dream that better days will come.

According to the second picture we are like prisoners who

have been imprisoned so long that now when any of them seems to speak of the outside world and says, perhaps, 'The sun is shining' he means only that in his mirror the sun shines, that his sound machines will give a sound as of voices saying, 'Yes, the sun is shining.' In such a case each prisoner has direct knowledge of what he claims is so when he says, for instance, that the sun is shining. For now he means only something about what his mirrors and other instruments show, will show, or would show. According to McTaggart's second account of our knowledge of the material world we are like the prisoners in the second case. When we say, 'This is champagne not vinegar' what we mean is something about the programme of sensations we may expect?

But now what is this second account of our knowledge of the material world? Is it not the same as that which Russell offers us when he says that material things are logical constructions out of sense data,[1] is it not the same as that which the logical analyst offers us when he says that when we speak of material things and say, for instance, 'This is champagne not vinegar' what we mean can be analysed into a complicated statement about what sensations we may expect.

McTaggart it is true does not come down firmly in favour of this account; indeed I should say that upon the whole he gives the impression that statements about sensations are not related to conclusions about material things as statements about individual men are related to conclusions about the statistical construction, the average man. Upon the whole he gives the impression that premisses about sensations or sense-data are related to conclusions about material things as premisses about pictures in a mirror are related to conclusions about what is pictured except that we have never turned to what is pictured. But this leaves it true that he is concerned with the same question as that which concerned the logical analysts, namely, 'Are statements about material things reducible to statements about our sensations or do they refer to something over and above our sensations?'

It is not my aim to discuss which of these models of the logical character of statements about material things is correct, nor to wonder whether perhaps they are both unsatisfactory

[1] Russell, *Our Knowledge of the External World*, p. 101.

and, perhaps, both helpful. No, my aim at the moment is to say this: read over what McTaggart says. Does he at any point rely upon some premiss which though true could conceivably have been false? Does it not now appear that if we look not at what traditional philosophers said about philosophy, nor at the forms of words in which they couched their questions and their answers, but at the procedure they adopted in reaching their answer forms then we see that what they did was after all different only in air and in guise from what is done by their logico-analytic successors. Their aim appeared to be different, but their proceedings were fundamentally the same. True, they preserved the air and guise of specially cautious scientists seeking to ascertain what is actual, not merely what is possible; but this was only a disguise for a procedure as purely *a priori* as that of the purest student of the structure of the possible, the most detached analyst of the abstract. And the analytic procedure, as we have already noticed, differs from that of those who ask not for the analysis of propositions but for the translation of sentences only in the openness with which the last appeal is allowed to appear as an appeal to the usage of words. Nor is this fundamental concern with the usage of words diminished when, no longer obsessed by equation or translation, we ask at last not for the definition but for the description of the usage of words.

But now, alas, we seem to have lost nothing only because we never had it, seem to have lost only an illusion, the illusion that somehow philosophy played some part in revealing the actual, and that not merely the actual use of words but the actual state of things which the use of words in everyday life, in history, in science, in law, purports to represent. That idea it now seems was all illusion.

Consider a somewhat parallel case. The statements 'Two and two always make four', 'Seven and five always make twelve' may at first seem to be statements which tell us about what actually happens in nature. Indeed teachers sometimes introduce these statements in such a way that a child may naturally think that they are established by experiments with beads, marbles, and the rest, and that they would be false were these experiments not to turn out as they do. It is only later that the child learns that these mathematical statements are statements which could not have been false no matter what had happened. They are not statements which would be shown to be false were we to drop two beads into a box and then two more and then upon opening the box find seven. Such a miraculous sequence of events would show only that we had been wrong in thinking that beads never breed other beads; it would not prove that two and two do not make four. When one says 'If there are two and two then there are four' one is not saying of two possible states of affairs that whenever one is actual the other is also, as one is when one says 'If you drink this you will recover.' But if one is not doing this when one says 'Two and two—that mean four' what is one doing? Is one saying 'The words "Two and two" mean the same as the word "Four" '? When one says 'If there are a dozen there are twelve, if there are two dozen there are twenty-four' is one saying 'the expression "a dozen" means the same as "twelve" '? Sometimes—but only when one is teaching the meaning of the word 'dozen' to someone who does not know its meaning, not when one is making the mathematical statement 'Two dozen, that means there are twenty-four.' One is making the mathematical statement only when one is *not* teaching, or even reminding oneself or another of the meaning of the expression 'a dozen'. It begins to seem as if one is making a mathematical statement only when one is saying nothing. What can be the point of making a mathematical statement, and in particular how can the making of it ever be of any use in apprehending the actual?

Let us think. When, in what circumstances, does one find it worth while to make a mathematical statement? Suppose someone knows that there are thirty-four guests at her party and can see set out three groups of glasses, in each group three rows with four glasses in each row. Still she is worried as to whether she has enough glasses. 'Look', you say, 'In each lot three rows of four. Three fours is a dozen. Three dozen means thirty-six. Thirty-six is thirty-four and two extra.' Her face clears. Your mathematical talk has not been useless. It has helped to set in a new light an actual situation, it has helped in reviewing an actual situation. The same effect *might* have been obtained without making any mathematical statement. You might have said: 'There are three groups and in each group there are three rows of four glasses. There are three dozen glasses. There are thirty-six glasses. There are thirty-four glasses and two extra.' Had you done this you would have made only statements which though true could have been false. Each later statement presents only what has already been presented in the one before it, but each later statement *presents differently* what has already been presented. Suppose one says, 'Indigenous, at Epsom, covered 5 furlongs in 55.0 seconds, so he travelled for more than half a mile at rather over 40 miles an hour.' The second description of this colt's performance omits ·part of the information provided by the first, but apart from that the second description may enable one readily to grasp the affinities and differences between his performance and that of locomotives, automobiles, cyclists, in a way in which the description in terms of furlongs may not. One may review an actual situation by redescribing it without making any mathematical or logical statement. But in fact we sometimes find it helpful to insert mathematical and logical statements which are all hypothetical and make no declaration as to what is actually the case and further are not dependent upon what actually happens in the way in which 'If you deprive rats of vitamin B they lose condition' is. For instance, one may say '5 furlongs in 55.0 seconds is over 40 miles an hour' or 'If anything covers 5 furlongs in 55.0 seconds then its average speed is over 40 miles an hour.' In saying this one prepares oneself to review actual situations, or, to put the thing another way, one reviews possible situations. One may do this with an eye to reviewing an actual situation which is already before one. But one may do it without much expecting ever to come upon a situation of the sort one reviews. For instance, I may say 'If I earned a salary of twenty thousand a year I should be earning wages of about £380 a week.' It may entertain me to review this possibility, to try to realize better what it would be like, even though I do not expect the possibility to become an actuality. In short with such statements one reviews the possible.

Here then in mathematical statements we have statements which at first appear to be telling us about what in fact happens in nature like the statements 'There is no smoke without fire' or 'Faint heart never won fair lady', and then turn out to be independent of what actually happens in nature, turn out to be nothing but words in which we review the possible. But such review of the possible may at any time serve us in reviewing the actual, for at any time the possible may become actual.

Mathematical and logical statements review the possible only on quite conventional lines. One may review the possible upon unconventional lines. For instance, someone may say: 'Suppose that on several occasions two men dream very vividly but very differently. Suppose that no research into the past, however careful and extended, reveals a hidden circumstance sufficient to explain why the one dreams as he does and the other as he does. Suppose, however, that the dream of each exactly and vividly portrays events which happen to him the following day. In such a case would not the explanation of the dreams lie not in what went before them but in what came after? But can the explanation of an event lie in what happens after it?' This question is not one to be settled by investigating nature. One might for a moment be tempted to call it a verbal question. But it is not a question of linguistic fact as to what people would say, nor a question of linguistic policy—'Shall we call an associated but future difference an "explanation"?' It is a question in which we frame and guide our efforts to view, to review, to contrast, to assimilate, to differentiate the shocking possibility we contemplate. Hitherto whenever we have been mystified because on one occasion an event occurred and on another occasion it did not, diligent research has always revealed a difference in what went before. In the case of the dreams we have imagined this would not be so. In face of such a shock we might feel our faith in science and order tremble, and then, looking at the situation again in the light of a modified notation, we might find our faith in science and order restored in a wider form. For looking not only at what goes before events but also at what comes after we might find a justification, not for the old faith that for every difference between two states of affairs there is always a difference in their present or past surroundings, but for the wider faith that for every difference between any two states of affairs there is always a difference *somewhere* in their surroundings, present, past, *or future*. At any moment such purely fanciful and also unconventional reviews of an extraordinary possibility may be needed by those concerned with the actual. For sometimes nature pulls a rabbit from a hat and makes our dreams come true.

Again someone may review unconventionally not some extravagant possibility but some familiar possibility. Sometimes we may be concerned not so to prepare ourselves for the extraordinary that we shall not be unable to 'take it in' when it occurs but to revive or renew our apprehension of possibilities so ordinary that when they are actual we hardly bother to take them in. Christ's story of the good Samaritan was not a story of some unparalleled incident. The point of the story lay in Christ's question 'Who was neighbour to him who fell among thieves? When dramatists, poets, novelists, present to us possible situations and give us a new view of these situations they do not assert, like historians, that such situations have actually occurred. They review the possible. But such review of the possible leads to a new view of the actual whenever and in so far as that reviewed as possible becomes actual.

So far so good. Words which make no statement as to the actual but merely review the possible may at any moment aid our apprehension of the actual.

Now what about metaphysical philosophy? Unquestionably metaphysics puts in a different light certain sorts of possible incidents and undoubtedly such incidents often occur. For instance, when a metaphysical philosopher says that questions as to good and evil are questions of taste, or questions as to how we feel, this puts in a new light what one does if and when one asks a moral question. Such an account of what one is doing if one asks a moral question represents a person who asks, for instance, 'Would it be wrong to go?' as more like than we had ever imagined to one who asks 'Would we feel guilty if we went?' Perhaps this account of moral questioning distorts it. Perhaps another metaphysical philosopher says, 'No, if someone asks "Would it be wrong to go?" then he is usually asking for further information as to what the present circumstances are, as to what are the facts of the case. It is only when no further question of fact remains that the words "Would it be wrong?" put to the hearers a question as to what his sentiments are towards going.' Perhaps a third philosopher says, 'No, this won't do. One who replies "It would be wrong" is not expressing his sentiments. His words are imperative and they mean "Don't go".' Perhaps a fourth philosopher says, 'No. You are all profoundly distorting the situation. The words "It would be wrong" are an answer to a question, and this question is not one which directly all the circumstances are known becomes a question of sentiment or no question at all, only a request for advice or orders. On the contrary, questions of right and wrong, good and evil are those which will be asked when we come to our last account. They will be argued before the Judge from whom no secrets are hid, they will be settled by the Great Accountant who makes no mistakes and whose books omit no liability and no asset. When an accountant calls a man bankrupt or declares him solvent his voice may betray contempt or satisfaction; when one calls a man a sinner or declares him a saint one may be said hardly to mean what one says unless one not only grasps his affinity to a paradigm as when one calls a spade a spade, a greyhound a greyhound, but also feels towards him in a certain way. As meta-moralists we must note this; for as meta-moralists we are concerned with what is done by one who makes a moral judgement. But we must note also how, just as the question "Is he bankrupt?" may call for thought even after all the facts have been ascertained, so may the question "Is he a sinner?" An answer to the question "Is he a sinner?" commits the speaker to an attitude to reality in a way in which an answer to the question "Is he bankrupt?" does not. But this does not make it any less an instrument for apprehending reality.'

I am not concerned here to argue which account of moral questioning is right or better, nor even to argue that the whole of this piece of meta-morals leaves us with a better apprehension of what it is to be concerned with a moral question than that we had before the meta-moralists began their talk.

But I do submit that each account, for better or for worse, puts in a new light anyone who is concerned with a moral question and that the whole discussion does this too even if at the end of it one is no more and no less inclined to offer the word 'objective' or the word 'subjective' as adequate descriptions of the nature of such a question as 'Would it be wrong?' The fact that we use the same word as we did before the metaphysics began, or that we are still dissatisfied with both words, does not mean that we do not know any better whether and how such questions are subjective or objective. When counsel for the plaintiff and counsel for the defendant present conflicting views of a case, then if one listens only to one of them one may easily get a distorted view of the case. It may even happen that when one listens to both, one's view of the case is in some way less clear than it was before one had heard all the argument. But it will certainly be different. And even if one still gives the same answer as one gave before the case came up for consideration the apprehension which lies behind the answer is different from that which lay behind it before.

On the other hand while recognition of *a priori* truth in logic and mathematics throws light both on what happens when a statement of a certain sort is made and also on the situation described by that statement, recognition of *a priori* truth in metaphysics does not in this *double* way throw light on the actual. Suppose a mathematician says, 'To say that there are three times twelve things of a certain kind in a certain place is equivalent to saying that there are thirty-six things of that kind in that place.' Consideration of what the mathematician draws our attention to will throw a light both on what is being done if and when someone says, for instance, 'There are three times twelve glasses here' and also on the situation which this person describes. Suppose a metaphysical philosopher says, 'To say that a thing is sweet is very like and yet profoundly different from saying that to most creatures with a sense of taste it tastes sweet.' Consideration of what the metaphysician draws our attention to will throw a light on what is being done if and when someone says, for instance, 'This sherry is sweet', but it will throw little or no light on the situation which this person describes. We need to inquire the reason for this if we are to grasp the nature of metaphysical philosophy and the difference between it and logic and mathematics. But that inquiry must be left for another time.

We must also leave for another time an inquiry into the difference and the connection between metaphysical philosophy and another study which is also called philosophy and finds expression in such words as 'Continual disappointment can be avoided and contentment attained only by overcoming the will to live', 'Life is a tale told by an idiot', 'For goodness, growing to a pleurisy, dies in his own too-much.'

VII

G. E. Moore

I used to go to tea with Moore almost every week during term-time until he went into hospital. After tea we used to have some philosophical talk. The last question we discussed was this: 'When people used to say that the Sun moves and the Earth does not, were they mistaken, were they saying what was false?' I think that Moore raised this question because he had been reading someone who maintained that those who in former times said that the Sun moves and the Earth does not were not saying what was false. I suggested that there is some reason to say that one who says 'the Sun appears to be sinking behind those trees, but it is not because it does not move' is not using the words "sinking" and "moving" in the usual sense; that there is some reason to say that one who in response to the question 'is the Sun already sinking behind the hills?' answers 'yes' is not saying what is false; and that one who, describing the behaviour of a child on a journey by train, says 'he never moved' is not saying what is false. Moore was interested in these considerations but he did not feel satisfied that the difficulty raised was cleared up, and, as I remember, at the end of this discussion he said something like this. 'But still, surely those who now say that the Sun is not moving and that the Earth is, are using the word "moving" in the same sense as that in which it was used by those who said that the Sun is moving and that the Earth is not.'

Nevertheless, it was Moore who said to me (I think it was when we were discussing the same matter a week later) 'There is a difficulty about saying that one who says of one of these chairs that it is not moving, is saying something false' or words to that effect.

I think that in this discussion, of which I have given an incomplete and very bare outline, are some things very characteristic of Moore.

Moore himself has said (*Philosophy of G. E. Moore*, p. 14), 'What has suggested philosophical problems to me is things which other philosophers have said about the world or the sciences'. Moore's work was often prompted by someone's asserting or appearing to assert that every proposition of a certain sort is false, when Moore believed that many propositions of that sort are true and known to be true. Moore did not hold that philosophy is analysis (*Philosophy of G. E. Moore*, p. 660, and *Some Main Problems of Philosophy*, p. 204). We know too that, though Moore would sometimes put a question as to whether one expression has the same meaning as another or as to whether in certain circumstances we would or would not use a certain expression, he would have denied that he was primarily concerned with questions about words.

What one may more easily miss I think is this: it is possible to discuss the analysis or the logical character of a type of statement or apparent statement, and to be indifferent to the truth or falsehood of these statements, and indifferent also to whether or no these statements have ever in fact been made or are still made. Moore was far from being indifferent to either of these matters. I believe that Moore's passionate desire to reach a correct analysis and to make clear the incorrectness of an incorrect analysis came in no small part from a feeling that an incorrect analysis of statements of a given type will, if one accepts it, tend to distort one's apprehension of what is being done when such a statement is in fact made, and may even hinder, at least temporarily, one's recognition of the truth or falsehood of what is being asserted. When I once said to Moore 'Those philosophers who have said that Matter does not exist did not mean to deny that you have two hands or a watch in your pocket', he reached down from his shelves MacTaggart's *Some Dogmas of Religion* and pointed to the words 'The result is that matter is in the same position as the Gorgons or the Harpies. Its existence is a bare possibility to which it would be foolish to attach the least importance, since there is nothing to make it at all preferable to any other hypothesis however wild'. Moore thought that I was not recognizing what had been done by MacTaggart and other philosophers and that I was failing to recognize the falsehood of (or in) what they had been asserting. He believed that, to say the least, they had been failing to recognize how far different is the position of hands, watches, chairs and tables from that of the Gorgons and the Harpies. And I submit that when Moore opposed the doctrine that material things are logical constructions out of sense-data he felt that this doctrine, even if it is in itself purely logical, when applied to those occasions on which a person does make a statement about a material thing, encourages one to think that he is merely doing one thing when in fact he is doing another. And didn't Moore also feel that this mistaken notion of what is being asserted when someone makes a statement about a material thing is still associated with an inadequate recognition of the truth of what is being asserted when the statement is true? (See *Some Main Problems of Philosophy*, p. 206).

The questions of analysis to which Moore gave most attention were questions whose answers would throw light on how we know propositions which some philosophers have said we do not know. This perhaps helps one to grasp how Moore's questions of analysis are connected with traditional philosophical questions which at least do not appear to be questions of analysis (*Some Main Problems of Philosophy*, p. 25).

If anyone put to Moore a very general question such as 'How is the conflict between Science and Common Sense to be resolved?', he would often respond by taking an instance or instances of the sort or sorts of statement giving rise to the problem and considering the problem in those instances. He would do this even when he did not feel in doubt as to what statements were referred to in the general question. For instance, when considering the meaning of 'Time is unreal', he writes 'But if you try to translate the proposition into the concrete, and to ask what it *implies*, there is, I think, very little doubt as to the sort of thing it implies. The moment you try to do this, and think what it really comes to, you at once begin thinking of a number of different kinds of propositions, all of which plainly must be untrue, if Time is unreal. If Time is unreal, then plainly nothing ever happens before or after anything else; nothing is ever simultaneous with anything else; it is never true that anything is past; never true that anything will happen in the future; never true that anything is happening now; and so on' (*Philosophical Studies*, p. 209).

It is well known that this move to the concrete was characteristic of Moore's philosophical thinking. But I believe it is still worth considering why this sort of move is so valuable. Isn't it a sort of move which Wittgenstein carried further, much further? Is it perhaps that the revival of a particular case is not just a means to finding an answer to a general question, or to resolving a riddle, but is a part of what in philosophy we aim at, a renewed view of the manifold of particular cases covered by our general terms. (Compare *Some Main Problems of Philosophy*, p. 205, and also *Philosophy of G. E. Moore*, p. 25, ' . . . stories, whether purporting to be true or avowedly mere fiction, have a tremendous fascination for me.') Such a renewed view of a classified manifold is sometimes reached by a process in which some people propound and defend, and others attack, a description, a statement, which is very strange, if not preposterous.

Moore, over the years, gave a great deal of attention to statements which are very paradoxical; this attention was most critical. 'When a man says that something is *really* so, we know it isn't'. Moore said this or something very like it in the course of a lecture he was giving many years ago. But though Moore was very outspoken, he was very patient. Consider his examination (1910–11) of what seemed to him the 'monstrous proposition' that Time is unreal (*Some Main Problems of Philosophy*, Chap. XI), of the doctrine that reality is spiritual, that *esse* is *percipi*, that all relations are internal (*Refutation of Idealism*, *Internal and External Relations*, 1919–20). The view that material things are logical constructions out of sense-data is a view about the analysis of a class of statements. As such, Moore would have said, it does not conflict with Common Sense like the 'view' that Matter does not exist. Nevertheless, it is a view about the meaning of statements made every day which, when it is introduced to non-philosophers, is very often regarded with a suspicion not unlike that which they feel when told that Matter doesn't exist. Moore, I think, always felt this sort of suspicion of this 'view'. But no one will deny that he gave it the most careful consideration when, in lecture after lecture in the twenties, he sought the analysis of 'this is a blackboard'; Moore in these lectures, as always, pursued the truth with an incisive and passionate honesty which none who heard him will forget. In later years he thought very carefully over the very strange statement that the propositions of mathematics are rules of grammar.

In short, although Moore was quite prepared to call false or unfounded what he thought he could see to be false or unfounded, he had a respect for what others had to say, and would give it his undivided attention while he thought that it might be true in some sense which he had not understood, or that there might be reasons for it which he had not considered. And although he was so much occupied with analytic, or abstract, questions, he was never indifferent to the influence of these upon an apprehension of the actual. And although, like other philosophers, he was concerned with the truth and falsehood of extremely general statements, it was his habit to test these by a careful examination of at least one of the particular cases they covered. He sought order, he wished to know whether what is true of this is also true of that; but he never lost that power and that desire to see each thing for what it is which has been remarked in great scientists and is present in great artists, poets, novelists. Here I think of Tolstoy's description in *Anna Karenina* of a shooting expedition in the evening, in *The Cossacks* of the grape harvest and of the death of the Chechen by the river.

Things as they are are often hard to face. We are often driven to distort them and this may lead to a distrust of what is said and an inability to see what is there, like that which overcomes a child when he finds those about him saying what is not true, and then, perhaps, begins himself to join in the conspiracy. There are those who attack our illusions; but often we feel that they in bitterness again distort reality. In spite of the forces which make for falsehood, we are still able to recognize one who can and will speak the truth, not blind to what we must regret, but still able to see things—some great, some small— which may bring happiness and can be shared. Moore was like this not only as a philosopher but as a man.

VIII

Ludwig Wittgenstein, 1934-1937

I have no notes worth speaking of about what Wittgenstein was saying in the years 1934, 1935, 1936 and 1937, when I attended his lectures and he talked to me about philosophical questions. I am relying on memory. As I remember, when I first went to a lecture by him, he was talking about the question, 'What is it to understand a general term, such as "plant"?' (See the first pages of the Blue Book.) He studied the cases in which we say of someone, 'He understands', 'He knows the meaning', 'He is being taught the meaning', 'After all he doesn't know the meaning', 'I know the meaning', and so on. This led to his emphasizing the point he expressed by, 'We have the idea that the several instances of a general concept all have something in common' (See the Blue Book.) (The concepts of 'understanding' and of 'having a meaning' are no exception.) He said that in applying the same word to several instances we mark a family resemblance—not the possession of something in common (as all ticket holders possess something in common—a ticket which matches a ticket I may hold in my hand as a sample, or as all alcoholic drinks possess something in common, in that from all of them may be distilled the essence of an alcoholic drink—alcohol).

This remark of his—that in applying the same word to several instances we mark a family resemblance and not the possession of something in common—was connected with a point which on one occasion at the Cambridge Moral Sciences Club he expressed in the words 'We have the idea that the point which on one occasion at the Cambridge Moral Sciences meaning of a word is an object'. This is connected with his saying 'Don't ask for the meaning, ask for the use', recommended at the Moral Sciences Club as a supplement to 'The meaning of a statement is the method of its verification'. And all this is connected with the question 'What happened when you understood?', and thus with his study of 'What happened while I was expecting so-and-so from 4 to 4.30?', and so with how much a question as to what happened when someone understood, believed, remembered, was reading, was coming to a decision, felt frightened, etc., is a matter of what happened before, and what will or would happen after, he understood, believed, etc., and with how our recognition of this is hindered by 'the idea of a mental mechanism', the hidden movements in which are these activities of the mind.

'We have the idea that the meaning of a word is an object' is also connected with 'The application (every application) of every word is arbitrary'. And this is connected with the question, 'Can you play chess without the queen?' (If I were asked to answer, in one sentence, the question 'What was Wittgenstein's biggest contribution to philosophy?', I should answer 'His asking of the question "Can one play chess without the queen?" '.) And all this about understanding is connected with his study of what it is to prove a thing, with the fact that people were often exasperated by his ending the discussion of a philosophical puzzle with 'Say what you like', with his saying to me on one occasion when I spoke of an unsuccessful philosophical discussion 'Perhaps you made the mistake of denying what he said', with his saying 'I hold no opinions in philosophy', and with his saying that he didn't *solve* philosophical problems, but *dissolved* them. At the same time he was always anxious to make people feel the puzzle—he was dissatisfied if he felt they had not done this.

The idea that the several instances of a general concept all have something in common is connected with the craving for a definition, 'the idea of an exact calculus', the model, the analogy, of an exact calculus. The fascination of this model for our language is connected with the fascination of models suggested in our language—the idea that the soul is a little man within, the model for our minds of the closed picture gallery, the model for causation of the wire connexion.

The substitution of the family resemblance model for the property-in-common model, and the substitution of 'Ask for the use' for 'Ask for the meaning' is linked with the procedure of explaining meaning by resenting not a definition but cases, and not one case but cases and cases. And this is linked with dealing with the philosophical, metaphysical, *can't* by presenting cases and cases.

Thus Wittgenstein said that if someone says 'One can't know the mind of another', one may ask 'Would you call this knowing the mind of another, or that, or that?' For example, one may ask 'Suppose a nerve of your body was joined to a nerve of Smith's, so that when someone stuck a pin into Smith you felt pain, would that be knowing, having, Smith's pain?' By this procedure, *either* (1) it is made clear what we would call 'knowledge of the mind of another', and hence what it would be to know the mind of another, *or* (2) it appears that we can't imagine what it would be to know the mind of another, and that not merely in the sense in which few people can form an image of a creature with twenty-two legs on one side and twenty-one on the other, but in the sense in which there is nothing the speaker would call 'knowing the mind of another' or 'feeling the pain of another'. If (1) is the case, then the person who says 'One can't know the mind of another' is saying of something which conceivably could happen, that it doesn't. Pigs don't fly. But if (2) is the case, then he has taken away the use of 'know what is in the mind of another' which we have been taught, and not provided us with a new use. And this makes meaningless his question 'Are other people automata?'.

I do not mean that such a procedure constituted Wittgenstein's whole treatment of the puzzle about knowledge of the mind of another. By no means. On the contrary, he emphasized the fact that in teaching the child the use of 'in pain' we not only point to others who are moaning, perhaps, but also pinch the child until it hurts, and say 'That's pain'. And with this two-fold teaching and learning goes a two-fold method of verification which makes 'He has toothache' very different from 'It goes in jerks'.

If one says that Wittgenstein showed metaphysical questions to be meaningless one must remember that he also said that what the Solipsist *means* is right. One must remember if one asks 'Can one attach a meaning to "Can one ever know that Smith is in pain, that there isn't a white rabbit between any two articles of furniture in this room"?' that one also asks 'Can one play chess without the queen?'.

II

A Feature of Wittgenstein's Technique

William James, at the beginning of his second lecture on *The Varieties of Religious Experience*, writes that 'Most books on the philosophy of religion try to begin with a precise definition of what its essence consists of'; and a little later says:

> The theorizing mind tends always to the over-simplification of its materials. This is the root of all that absolutism and one-sided dogmatism by which both philosophy and religion have been infested. Let us not fall immediately into a one-sided view of our subject but let us rather admit freely at the outset that we may very likely find no one essence, but many characters which may alternately be equally important to religion. If we should inquire for the essence of 'government', for example, one man might tell us it was authority, another submission, another police, another an army, another an assembly, another a system of laws; yet all the while it would be true that no concrete government can exist without all these things, one of which is more important at one moment and others at another. The man who knows governments most completely is one who troubles himself least about a definition which shall give their essence. Enjoying an intimate acquaintance with all their particularities in turn, he would regard an abstract conception in which these were unified as a thing more misleading than enlightening.

And in his first lecture he says:

> To understand a thing rightly we need to see it both out of its environment and in it,

and

> it always leads to a better understanding of a thing's sig-
> nificance to consider its exaggerations and perversions, its
> equivalents and substitutes and nearest relatives elsewhere.

A Wittgenstein said: 'We have the idea that the meaning of a word is an object.' He spoke of the craving for generality, of the contemptuous attitude towards the particular case. He said: 'The idea that in order to get clear about the meaning of a general term one has to find the common element in all its applications has shackled philosophical investigation, for it has not only led to no result, but has also made the philosopher dismiss as irrelevant the concrete cases which alone could have helped him to understand the usage of the general term. When Socrates asks the question "What is knowledge?" he does not regard it as even a preliminary answer to enumerate cases of knowledge.'

These specifications and reformulations help us to know what he meant, but as he himself would have insisted, they don't take us far enough. The best way to teach a child the meaning of money is to show him what it will buy, and what it will not. We can't tell what a man means, we can't tell what Wittgenstein means, until we have faced the laborious job of finding what in innumerable incidents he refers to. This takes time.

B A first and very natural response when someone says 'We have the idea that the meaning of a word is an object' is to reply: 'Do you mean that we think that the meaning of a word is an object like a house, or a stone, or a cloud, or a block of ice? If so you are quite wrong. We haven't any such idea any more than we have the idea that the soul is a ghost or a bird, or the idea that causal connections are made of string. Or do you mean that we have the idea that the meaning of a word is an object, an entity, of a peculiar kind, not concrete but abstract, not subject to decay but timeless. If so, isn't that idea correct? We speak with the help of certain metaphors. We speak of the soul as within a body, as inhabiting a body, as leaving its tenement of clay; we speak of the likenesses between things in terms of the characteristics they *possess*, of the qualities *in* them. But what's the harm in these metaphors? What is the evidence that normal people or even philosophers are deluded by these metaphors?'

C The first part of the answer is this. It is notorious that philosophers spend much time on certain questions, and that though it isn't true that they make no progress with them, the whole business is or was in an unsatisfactory state. Philosophers, professional and amateur, often amaze, bewilder, and even alarm us and themselves by saying that we don't know things which we had all along thought we knew. We may as soon as they stop talking endeavour to smother our fears by saying 'It's all nonsense'. And we can do this the better because among the philosophers are some who say this same thing, namely, 'It's all nonsense'. Besides, though there have always been sceptical philosophers who say that we don't know, there have always been others who say that what the sceptics say is false, and that we do know. And this dispute has gone on not merely for hours, not merely for years, but for centuries. Isn't that perhaps because the parties to the dispute don't know what they are talking about? And when one recalls philosophical controversy this suspicion is confirmed. A question in accountancy may baffle expert accountants for hours, a question as to the causes of malaria or of cancer may baffle expert investigators for years. Experts may differ and it may take time to settle which is right. But though experts often differ as to an answer, they don't differ as to what the general character of the procedure appropriate to their questions is, or not nearly as much as philosophers do. I mustn't exaggerate. Sometimes, especially of late years, when philosophers disagree they yet do proceed on the same lines in settling the issue. And then very often the issue is settled. Also, it isn't only philosophers who carry on disputes in a way which makes one feel that there is no agreement as to what is to count in favour of one answer and what in favour of another. Some political disputes smack of this—are they concerned with what *should* be so, or with what *would* be so if this or that were done? Still, it is especially among philosophers that one gets the impression of a game of cross questions and crooked answers. Among them, and I am one of them, one very often and very strongly gets the feeling 'They aren't talking the same language, they aren't at all talking the same language.'

D Amongst the differences between players of the philosophic game which make one feel inclined to say they aren't playing the same game though they don't realize this is one very large one which I want to emphasize. It's this. Some philosophers have said in so many words that philosophical questions, or truly philosophical questions, are concerned with the meanings of words, or the logical structure of the propositions we express by the sentences we utter. For instance, Professor Ayer said in *Language, Truth and Logic*, p. 50: 'If the philosopher is to uphold his claim to make a special contribution to the stock of our knowledge, he must not attempt to formulate speculative truths. . . . He must, in fact, confine himself to works of clarification and analysis of a sort we shall presently describe.' And of course many who say this sort of thing proceed accordingly. Philosophers of this sort have been or might be called 'logico-analytical philosophers', or 'logico-mathematical philosophers', or 'philosophers of the linguistic school'. There are sometimes differences between philosophers who say that philosophical questions are concerned with the meanings of words, and those who say that philosophical questions are logical, and you may feel that you are not very clear about what either of them means. But at least they agree in this, and at least this much is clear: both wish to insist on a close affinity in a certain respect between philosophical questions and logical and mathematical questions. Both wish to insist that philosophical questions are akin to logical and mathematical questions in a certain respect very characteristic of logical and mathematical questions. It is this. Without denying for a moment that logical and mathematical truths in some way help us when we are trying to learn and to grasp the way things happen, we must remark that the truth and falsehood of mathematical and logical statements does not depend on what happens to come about. Come what may, $2+2 = 4$. Come what may, $2+2$ will never equal 5. It never has, and it never will, and it never could. Maybe in some golden age when you put into a basket two eggs and then two more you could then pull out five. Maybe. But tall stories don't interest the mathematician; anyway they don't alarm him, they only amuse him. For his point is that while, when, and in so far as, there are two things of a certain sort and two more then there couldn't but be four, it's nonsense to talk of there being five. And it's the same with logic. Come what may, if all men are mortal and you and I are men, then we are mortal too. The inevitable is unshaken by the accidental, the timeless untouched by the temporal.

E Now are philosophical questions like that? Are they questions as to what could or could not have been so and not at all questions as to what has been, is, or will be so though it might not have been? Take, for instance, the famous question 'Can one ever really, directly, know what is in the mind of another?' Is this question like a logical, mathematical question in that it is a question as to whether something conceivably could happen, if not in this world then in a better? Or is it a question as to what actually happens, like the question 'Can one live for four days without water?'

F One might hope that this seemingly simple question as to the character of a certain question would be easy to answer. But it is not. There are two sources of difficulty. Suppose someone asks 'What is the character of the Englishman? Is he simple and honest like a bull-dog, or is he very foxy?' It is not easy to answer this question. In the first place, there are Englishmen and Englishmen and Englishmen. Some are comparatively simple and honest like dogs, some are *very* foxy, and many are mixed. In the second place, even in the case of an individual Englishman it is not as easy to say what character he possesses as it is to say whether he possesses a watch of gold or any other object. We may of course guess that a man possesses a watch from the many occasions on which he arrives on time for pleasant appointments and ten minutes late for unpleasant ones. But besides observing and remembering those incidents in a man's life which may well be due to his possession of a watch, there is a quicker and surer way of telling whether he has a watch or any other object, namely, looking to see. But with his character, his motives, and his meaning, there is not. There is no better and surer way of ascertaining what character a man possesses or what motives drive him than that of observing and remembering those incidents in his life which are due to his possession of that character. To study these is to study his character and the driving forces of his life.

We could the better cope with the first difficulty, namely, the varieties among Englishmen, if, though numerous, they fell into one or two definite types, like the horses of a county where there are only heavy draught horses and racehorses, and nothing betwixt and between. But they don't, any more than Frenchmen or Americans do. The consequence is that we have to keep in mind certain real or imaginary individuals such as Bull-Dog Drummond and Mr. Sherlock Holmes or perhaps Mr. Lloyd George, who was, I think, called the Welsh fox, and describe other individuals as being like, very like, rather like, or unlike, far from or near to these fixed stars who exhibit certain traits in extreme or in purity. Of course the manifold of human nature, and even of the Englishman's nature, has innumerable dimensions, and consequently the frame of reference calls for many pairs of stars. The study of human nature is endless. But this doesn't mean that nothing can be done, and novelists and psycho-analysts and others who study mankind keep on at the job.

Fortunately, questions about the characters of questions are not quite so difficult to deal with. But the same sort of difficulties arise. Our question was 'Is the question "Can one know what is in the mind of another?" a question as to what actually happens like the questions "Can one last for four days without water?" or "Are there people with clairvoyant powers?" or is it a question as to what conceivably could be the case like "Could one square the circle?"?'

Having in mind the first difficulty in dealing with questions about the Englishman we are ready to notice much variety in the manifold of occasions which may be referred to by one who speaks of 'the question whether one can ever really know the mind of another'. There are many occasions on which someone says 'One can't really know or can't directly know what is in the mind of another' and explains why he says what he does, and these occasions may differ not merely in what is meant by the words used but in the type of statement which is being made. It may be that they are sometimes used to make a statement as to a matter of fact which might have been otherwise, and sometimes used to make a statement which if true could not have been false and if false could not have true. In order to grasp the character of the question raised or statement made on any *one* of these occasions we have to review the course of the discussion which forms what one might call the life history of that question on that occasion. In order to learn a man's character or his motives we cannot rely on his appearance or even on what he says. In order to learn what a man means we cannot rely on the form of words he uses nor even on what he says he means. The proof of the pudding is in the eating.

Suppose that when a person *A* asks 'Can one ever know what is in the mind of another?' it turns out that he is concerned with the correctness of all those stories, accounts, and figures which bear on the matter of whether it sometimes happens that one person knows what is in the mind of another without being able to see him or hear what he says or observe what he does, and that he is concerned to investigate these phenomena and add to this evidence. It seldom happens, I think, that a discussion which centres round the question 'Can one ever really know the mind of another?' proceeds purely as if the question were the question of fact 'Are there people with telepathic powers?' But *sometimes* such discussions approach this. The more they do, the more they are scientific and concerned with what actually happens.

Sometimes, however, one who says 'One can never know what is in the mind of another' is not concerned with the exotic facts which support the claim that there are people with telepathic powers. For instance, when Matthew Arnold in *Isolation* says 'We mortal millions live alone,' he is not concerned with exotic facts which support the claim that there are people with telepathic powers. He is concerned with facts familiar to us all even though we ignore them. He is much less calling upon us to investigate incidents we have never come upon than to reflect upon those we have. And here we may think of Newton. Here we may remember how Einstein, when astronomers were hurrying to check his theory, remarked to Bertrand Russell, 'Whatever they find, it's a damn good theory.' Further observation was not irrelevant to the theories of Newton and Einstein, but we are apt to forget how much they called for thought, for reflection upon phenomena which had already been observed. What is more, their theories called for reflection involving a modification in our ideas, our idea of space and time, our idea of the action of one thing upon another. They spoke paradoxically. And so of course did Arnold when he said that each of us is alone really. He was concerned with something more difficult to remedy than what we usually count as being alone, with something more difficult to reach than what we usually count as meeting other people at a large luncheon party or a family breakfast. Because what he says is at once reflective and paradoxical, so that the thought it calls for runs counter to our usual habits, we may perhaps call his words philosophical. But if we do we must remember that, like one who says that nothing is really solid or that everything is bound to everything by invisible bonds, he is still concerned to show us the actual in contrast with what is conceivable. He speaks in *The Buried Life* of times when, as he puts it, 'a hand is laid on ours . . . and what we mean we say and what we would we know.' This is why I say that even though that of which he speaks is seldom or never attained, it is not something which, like parallel lines that meet, *could* not have been.

Even Proust is not plainly and definitely concerned only with what is absolutely inevitable when he writes

> . . . it was she who first gave me the idea that a person does not (as I had imagined) stand motionless and clear before our eyes with his merits, his defects, his plans, his intentions with regard to oneself exposed on his surface, like a garden at which, with all its borders spread out before us, we gaze through a railing, but is a shadow, which we can never succeed in penetrating, of which there can be no such thing as direct knowledge, with respect to which we form countless beliefs, based upon his words and sometimes upon his actions, though neither words nor actions can give us anything but inadequate and, as it proves, self-contradictory information—a shadow behind which we can alternately imagine, with equal justification, that there burns the flame of hatred and of love.

In his words we detect the influence of professional philosophers. But in his words we feel still the air of an old regret, regret for what might have been.

Does it ever happen that one who says 'One can never know what is in the mind of another' is concerned with what it would be as senseless to lament as it is to lament that one cannot draw a circle that is square? Are there among the discussions which centre round the words 'Can one ever really know what is in the mind of another?' some in which the issue in no way depends on what could conceivably have been otherwise?

The answer is: Yes. For some such discussions approximate to the following model:

A. How odd is mind.
Q. What's so odd about mind?
A. It's so accessible and at the same time so elusive.
Q. How d'you mean?
A. Well, one can know very well what's in one's own mind, and know well enough what's in the outside world, but one can't really know what's in the mind of another.
Q. How d'you mean?
A. When there is a question as to whether one feels cold one can answer better than anyone else. When there is a question as to whether it is cold one can answer as well as anyone else. But when there is a question as to whether someone else feels cold one can't answer as well as he.
Q. How d'you mean?
A. When there is a question as to whether one feels cold one's feeling of cold gives one better reason to answer Yes than does a like feeling give to anyone else. When there is a question as to whether it is cold one's feeling of cold gives one as good reason to answer Yes as does a like feeling give to anyone else. But when there is a question as to whether someone else feels cold one's feeling of cold does not give one as good reason to answer Yes as does a like feeling give him.
Q. When is a question a question as to whether one feels cold, when is a question a question as to whether it is cold, and when is a question a question as to whether someone else feels cold?
A. A question is a question as to whether one feels cold when one's feeling of cold gives one better reason to answer Yes than does a like feeling give to anyone else. A question is a question as to whether it is cold when one's feeling of cold gives one as good reason to answer Yes as does a like feeling give to anyone else. A question is a question as to whether someone else feels cold when one's feeling of cold does not give one as good reason to answer Yes as does a like feeling give him.

Q. Is it then so odd that mind is so accessible and so elusive?

In this discussion it comes out that the so-called Sceptic does not at any point refer to anything which could have been otherwise. Mind indeed is odd, but there is no more anything odd about its oddity than there is about the oddity of irrational numbers or of odd numbers. The 'asymmetrical' logic of statements about the mind is a feature of them without which they would not be statements about the mind, and that they have this feature is no more a subject suitable for regret than the fact that lines if truly parallel don't meet.

More than this comes out of this discussion. For in it there emerges not merely the result that what the Sceptic means could not have been false, but also what it is he means. And both these results are obtained not by asking him to define his terms, to reformulate what he says, but by a process which leads him to illustrate in instances what it is he refers to. A person who says 'One can never really know the mind of another' may add 'I mean, one can never know directly the mind of another, never observe, never be acquainted with, his experiences, his sense-data, his own immediate experience.' But these reformulations leave us still in difficulties. And if he coins a phrase and speaks of 'the asymmetrical logic' of statements about minds then, though his words make it clear that he is concerned to remark some inevitable feature of statements about minds, we are still not clear what this feature is without instances of statements which are about minds contrasted with instances of statements which are not about minds but about the material world, pairs of statements which are as like as possible except in the feature to be illustrated.

Take another instance. The statements of pure mathematics have a familiar but remarkable feature: they are true no matter what happens. The feature I refer to in this way has been referred to in many other ways. The truths of mathematics, it has been said, can be known by thought alone, can be derived from self-evident principles. The questions of pure mathematics, it has been said, can be answered from an understanding of the terms involved. And, more paradoxically, it has been said that the statements of pure mathematics are not really statements but rules as to the use of words, or again that they all tell us nothing.

The very variety of these descriptions of the peculiar character of the questions and statements of pure mathematics suggests that though we have always had some appreciation of their character, that appreciation has not been quite satisfactory. And isn't it true that we may be puzzled by such questions as 'What is it for the answer to a question to be self-evident, or obtainable by thought alone? How can one know that what a person says is true merely by knowing what he means by the words he uses? And if the statements of mathematics could not be false no matter what happened how can they tell us anything as to what happens? And if they tell us nothing as to what happens how can they help us in any every-day or scientific enquiry as to what happens?'

In spite of the inadequacy and even deceptiveness of the various descriptions which have been given we must allow that in the course of time an apprehension of the difference between armchair questions which can be answered by thought alone, and those questions which cannot be answered without experiment and observation, has improved. And I admit, that what philosophers have said in trying to describe the nature of mathematical questions has contributed to our better apprehension of that nature. What I want to do here is only this: to recall with emphasis what I think no one will deny, that the final testing of the merits of these descriptions lies always in applying them to instances.

But now if no one would deny this, why do I assert it; if everyone would admit it, why do I try to emphasize it? Because I believe that though everyone will admit that descriptions of the nature of mathematical enquiry should be tested by the consideration of instances of such enquiry, and even puts this advice into practice, nevertheless the consideration of instances is often *very perfunctory*. Too often the response to a proffered description of the nature of mathematical enquiry consists less in vigorous review of the instances that description purports to cover than it does in argument such as the following: 'You say that mathematical statements are not really statements. But surely they may be wrong or right, true or false.' Or 'You say that mathematical statements all say the same thing, namely, nothing. But then (*a*) how is it that they differ from one another, and (*b*) how can they be wrong or right?'

Without saying that this ratiocination gets us nowhere I do submit that it doesn't get us far, and certainly not where we want to be, namely, at an understanding of what was really meant by the philosopher who said these paradoxical things as to the place of mathematical enquiry in the manifold of all enquiry. In order to see whether his metaphor, his extravagant words, illuminate that position we need to bring before the mind, in lively detail, pictures, moving pictures, of people engaged upon a mathematical enquiry, and compare it with a film of one engaged upon an enquiry as like as possible yet still not mathematical—an enquiry perhaps about the actual habits of beads, pulleys, dice, not the habits of perfect celestial, timeless dice, pulleys, beads, but of their terrestrial, temporal copies. In this way we may come to see how misleading it is to describe statements about mathematical, perfect, pulleys and their faultless performance as statements about a species of pulley, and why one should represent mathematical statements as far nearer than we had realized to such statements as 'If a being were perfect he would be sinless.' And should we for a moment be tempted by the paradox 'Mathematical statements say nothing' to consider them all as bringing no more light than 'Sinless beings don't sin', then revival of instances will correct this misplacement, and still leave us the insight we won when instances reminded us how immune are mathematical statements, whether about the integers or the performance of systems of perfect pulleys, to all that happens in space and time.

The same procedure by instances which is needed when we are faced with such paradoxes as 'Mathematical statements say nothing' or the paradoxical pronouncement 'One can never know the mental, inner, world of another', is needed again when we are faced with the other old metaphysical paradoxes: 'One can never know the external physical world, but only our sensations of it,' 'One can never know the past,' 'One can never know anything beyond one's own sensations of the moment.'

I believe that if, faced with the extraordinary pronouncements of metaphysicians, we avoid asking them to define their terms, but instead press them to present us with instances of what they refer to contrasted with instances of what they do not refer to, then their pronouncements will no longer appear either as obvious falsehoods or mysterious truths or pretentious nonsense, but as often confusingly presented attempts to bring before our attention certain not fully recognized and yet familiar features of how in the end questions of different types are met. These are features without which the questions or statements of the type in question would not be themselves. And they are features which can seldom or never be safely or vividly brought to mind by the use of general terms.

When Wittgenstein said 'We have the idea that the meaning of a word is an object', when he spoke of our craving for a definition and of our contempt for concrete cases, he was not saying that these habits of 'abstract' thought always and everywhere mislead us. But he was claiming that too often when what we need is to come down towards the concrete, we don't, and that this especially hinders our philosophy, our metaphysics.

Others before Wittgenstein had warned us of 'abstract' thought. But Wittgenstein *showed* the danger of it in instance after instance. Kant said that examples are the go-cart of the human understanding. But this is not enough. Examples are the final food of thought. Principles and laws may serve us well. They can help us to bring to bear on what is now in question what is not now in question. They help us to connect one thing with another and another. But at the bar of reason, always the final appeal is to cases.

And this has application beyond the sphere of metaphysics. For if we now turn from the remote sphere of metaphysics and think of more normal enquiry directed upon the actual events in nature, in life, we shall find on occasion questions which cannot be answered, statements which cannot be tested, either by experiment and observation or by reasoning in general terms. And amongst them are some of those questions and statements which mean most to us, and most call for thought. When, for instance, Sartre says that love is a condition in which one person consumes another, or when someone says that devotion is an explosive mixture of hate and love, or that we are all much more haunted by what is past than we recognize, and more bankrupt of the power to live or to love than we allow, then these words call less for experiment than for thought. But thought too will fail us here if we think that all thought which carries us to the truth must be thought on lines as definable or at least as conventional as the thought of an accountant who assesses a firm's financial position, and forget how much it may be a matter of giving our minds to incidents and incidents, whether they be as familiar as the fall of an apple or as recondite as the Michelson-Morley experiment, or the disorder of a madman like poor Dr. Schreber.

X

Price's 'Thinking and Experience'

Professor H. H. Price's book *Thinking and Experience* is profound yet simple, far reaching yet down to earth. Price uses
the work of other thinkers and yet looks at the world of cats
and clouds and words and pictures for himself.

The book is far-reaching because it is concerned with all
efforts to understand things from the cat who hears a sound and
thinks it's a mouse to the man who reads an argument and
thinks he smells a fallacy. Each sort of incident referred to is very
familiar. And yet the whole book—for the book is a whole
which works steadily towards a climax—the book as a whole
shows us these incidents in a way in which we have not seen
them before.

The book is profound because Price is not content with a
description merely because it is not inaccurate. One may, like
the *Oxford Dictionary*, define a nation as 'a distinct race or
people having common descent, language or political institu-
tions'. But then just what amounts and mixtures of these
ingredients are necessary to make a nation? And besides, what
is it to be of a distinct race, what is it to have a common history?
In the same way one may define thinking as the implicit or
explicit use of concepts. But when we have done this we still
want to ask 'What is it to use a concept?' Again we may say
that when things resemble each other they 'share a characteristic', 'partake of the same quality'. But is this way of putting
things any better? Isn't it perhaps not so good?

Price takes us with him to notice the many little things that
go to make it true in a particular instance or group of instances
that here someone, some person or animal, is thinking, using its
wits, comparing this with that, noting affinities, resemblances,
characteristic features, qualities and relations. He moves from

one group of cases to another until our grasp of the relations between these families is a grasp of the whole society of occasions on which some person, animal or angel is thinking.

One who asks 'What is it to try to see the good and evil in the world?' must compare the thinking appropriate to 'Did I do wrong?' with other sorts of thinking, for instance, with the sort appropriate to 'Does this disgust me?' and also with the sort appropriate to 'Did I argue badly?' The work of such a 'meta-moralist' is not done until he has compared moral thinking with every other sort of thinking. Likewise one who asks 'What is it to think about mathematical matters?' compares the thinking appropriate to 'Is every even number the sum of two primes?' with every other sort of thinking. But though the meta-moralist and the meta-mathematician view the same manifold, the one arranges the light so that it is focused on one part of that manifold, the other arranges it so that it is focused on another part. Each is concerned to bring out the affinities between the points within the area with which he is primarily concerned but each is also concerned to bring out the contrasts between the points within that area and those outside it. Now one who asks not 'What is thinking about things of type so and so?' but, in general, 'What is thinking?' does not focus the light more upon one area of the manifold of thought than upon another. He is still concerned with the varieties of thought. But they are all varieties within the field with which he is primarily concerned, for in his case this is no less than the total manifold of thought, the unity and diversity in which he aims to grasp.

This is a big job, the widest, the most abstract, the most tail-catching job a philosopher can undertake. How does Price begin?

He begins by remarking that there is a great deal of recurrence or repetition in the world. The same colour recurs over and over again. Shapes repeat themselves likewise. The same quality characterizes different things, the same relation holds between different things. These qualities and relations, these characteristics he says have been called by some philosophers 'universals'. All this seems innocent enough. The word 'universals' is a little quaint but it's harmless surely. Where does the

trouble lie? Things resemble one another, things share characteristics, the same universal may be present in several things.
Where does mischief creep in? What mischief *can* creep in if
these new forms of words mean the same as the old? Let's
look again at what Price says. On p. 10 he writes 'Is it not just
an obvious fact about the world, something we cannot help
noticing whether we like it or not, that there *are* recurrent
characteristics? Now these recurrent characteristics have been
called by some philosophers universals', and in the next sentence
he says 'And the line of thought we have been pursuing leads
very naturally to the traditional Aristotelian doctrine of
'universalia in rebus', 'universals in things'.' Nevertheless on
the same page he writes 'The doctrine of universalia in rebus
may, of course, be misleading or gravely mistaken.' But how
can the doctrine be mistaken? For what is the doctrine but the
doctrine that there are universals in things, that there are
recurrent characteristics? And this, as Price says, is the obvious
fact.

So we are still left asking 'Where does the mischief come in?'
And may I say at once that it is no wilful secretiveness on
Price's part that makes it difficult to get at this. It just is extremely difficult to bring out what dangers lie in saying that
when two things are alike in some way then they have in them
the same universal, or share the same characteristic. It is
difficult because it is not incorrect to say this and what is more
by and large it makes no mischief to say this. The trouble is that
sometimes it makes mischief.

When does it do so? And what mischief does it make?
What are the dangers of the doctrine of universals? Or as
Price later puts it 'What are the dangers of the *terminology* of
universals, of qualities and relations?'

One danger, Price says (p. 11) is that universals may be regarded as a sort of things or entities. But what is a person like
when he is regarding universals or characteristics as entities?
Is he merely one who speaks of qualities, relations, characteristics, and of their being in things and possessed by things? But
surely we *all* talk like this. We speak of noticing the same
characteristics in one man that we have noticed in another, as
we speak of noticing in The Swan the same people we have

noticed in The Goat and Compass. But surely there is no harm in this old metaphor? Surely no one will think that the redness of a tomato is something in it as its juice is in it. As Price says, when we speak of the elasticity *possessed* by india-rubber, the red *in* a tomato, the blue *of* the sky, then the meaning of 'in', 'of', and 'possessed by' is easily exhibited by examples. And Price says that if our metaphors can be cashed quite easily by examples no harm whatever is done. The danger of the doctrine is *still* hidden.

On p. 13 Price provides a clue which takes us further though not far enough. He writes: 'When we say that a characteristic characterizes ever so many different objects, what we say is admittedly in some sense true. But would it not be clearer and closer to the facts if we said that all these objects resemble each other in certain ways? Is not this the rock bottom fact to which the Philosophy of Universals is drawing our attention when it uses this rather inflated language of recurrent characteristics?'

This helps us, for it suggests that the position is as follows: The ordinary man sometimes says such a thing as 'There is in her eyes an extraordinary brightness' and sometimes says 'She has eyes like stars'. He expresses no opinion as to which expression is clearer or closer to the facts. But the person who holds the philosophy of resemblances does. He insists that 'She has eyes like stars' is somehow clearer and closer to the facts. The person who holds the philosophy of universals does not agree. He even insists that on the contrary 'Her eyes possess an extraordinary brightness' is clearer and closer to the facts than 'She has eyes like stars'.

So far so good. But what is it for one form of words to be clearer and closer to the facts than another? 'Her eyes are very bright' or 'Her eyes possess an extraordinary brightness' is surely just as clear and close to the facts as 'Her eyes are like stars'. And if the point is that the second form of words, the simile, takes us 'nearer to the *rock bottom* facts' then we want very fully explained to us with plenty of examples what it is for one form of words to take us nearer to the rock bottom facts than does another.

If a metaphor, even when it does not involve falsehood, even when it does not mislead, may yet hinder clearness of vision of the rock bottom facts, we want it explained how this happens—in general, and in particular in the case of the metaphor 'In all these things is present the same feature, characteristic, universal'.

And Price does very little directly to explain this. He does something but not enough. He suggests that the terminology of universals is apt to be especially inadequate when a resemblance is only just enough to make it true that a certain universal is present. This is an important starting point. But he does not go far from it. He says (p. 13): 'The philosophy of universals may tend to make us think that the world is a more neat and tidy place than it is'. This is a pregnant statement. But he does not develop it. He passes instead to another matter—that of what it is to think that a thing is of a certain sort, what it is to have in mind a certain universal or concept. I must protest against this hasty abandonment of the job of explaining the dangers that lie in the valuable metaphor which we use whenever we speak of universals being in things, for the job of explaining the dangers that lie in the valuable metaphor which we use whenever we speak of universals coming before the mind.

Price might reply to my protest on these lines: 'I have devoted a whole book to setting out all that there is in thinking that a thing is of a certain sort, I have endeavoured to explain the dangers that lie in speaking of someone as seeing a universal, as inspecting a characteristic. Now anyone who has grasped the dangers that lie in such expressions as "So and so sees the common characteristic in these things" ought to be able to grasp the dangers that lie in such expressions as 'There is in these things a common characteristic".' There is a great deal in this reply.

It is true that the dangers that lie in these two metaphors, these two forms of expression, are *very* closely connected. But still they are not the same and also we need help in grasping this close connection. And Price does not give us that help. On the contrary he calls the metaphor involved in saying that someone *sees or inspects* a universal in different things a very dangerous metaphor (p. 325) while (p. 12) he makes light of the dangers of the metaphor involved in saying that a universal is in different things. He says that we can easily find examples to explain what is referred to by one who speaks of things having in them the same universal. But then so can we easily find examples to explain what is referred to by one who speaks of someone as inspecting a universal.

Again at the beginning of Chapter II Price speaks of the issue between the philosophy of universals and the philosophy of resemblance as an ontological question about the nature of the world, and he contrasts this with what he calls an 'epistemological question' about the nature of intelligence, about what it is to recognize a universal. A philosophical description of what it is for things to *be* white or black or whatever it is, is in a sense more directly concerned with the world than a philosophical description of what it is to *think* things white or black or whatever it is. But *neither* of them is about the world like a guess as to some matter of fact, neither is concerned with the unknown nature of the flora and fauna of the universe. It is true that a philosopher who reminds us of what it is to *think* a thing to he white is still no physiologist nor even a psychologist. But then it is also true that a philosopher who sets out what it is for things to *be* white is no physicist. Put the matter another way: If one who adopts the philosophy of universals is one who encourages by precept and practice a certain terminology which has advantages and dangers, then surely it is clearer to say so and then to say *what* the advantages and dangers of this terminology are.

However, there it is. Price's book is called *Thinking and Experience* and he is mainly concerned *not* with what it is for things to *be* of a certain sort but with what it is to *think* them to be of a certain sort. And he is concerned with this in a very 'disinterested' way. I mean he isn't concerned to bring out how an inadequate conception of what it is to think may in certain circumstances distort our thought. He just wants an adequate conception of thinking, whether this conception helps us to think better or not. He is a pure philosopher. He wants a fair and at the same time profound description of what it is for a cat, a man or an angel to have sense as well as senses. He tries to provide a correct, clear, and above all 'rock bottom' description of what it is to have a concept, to have before the mind a universal.

First he sets out what it is to recognize that a thing is of a certain sort, then what it is to think mistakenly that a thing is of a certain sort, then what it is to think of things of a certain sort even when no such thing is present, even when no such thing exists. He sets out too what it is to take a thing's being of a certain sort as a conclusive or partial sign of its being of a further sort. He sets out too how all or some of these things are done without words or images, with images but without words, with words but without images, with both words and images. Put it another way: Price reminds us of what it is for a man to recognize a smell as 'mousy' or a mouse as a mouse, what it is to mistake something for a mouse, to imagine a mouse, to speak or write about mice.

I can't summarize all he says. A summary of metaphysics is self-defeating, like a summary of a novel or a poem.

But I would like to make two comments which I think readers may find useful. First Price distinguishes between what he calls *primary recognition* that a thing is of a certain sort and *secondary recognition* that a thing is of a certain sort. If you recognize something you can see as white, that's primary recognition, because you are not taking what you can see as a sign of anything further. If you recognize something as snow or salt then that is secondary recognition because you are taking what you can see as a sign of something further. I believe this distinction is profoundly important. But I think Price hinders our grasping its importance by declaring that in primary recognition error is impossible, that it is not subject to verification. I think he is wrong here. It it true of course that one can hardly make a mistake as to whether what one sees with good eyes in a good light is white. But can't one make a mistake as to whether what one sees is a willow pattern plate? Can't one come to the conclusion that the picture which at first one thought brilliant is really rather pretentious, that the case which at first appeared to be one of negligence is not? In saying that only secondary recognition is susceptible of error Price weakens his own good work on primary recognition and is led to give an inadequate account of what happens when a person uses words to himself in his own reflections (see p. 198). It is my belief that it is especially in cases where we are trying to apprehend what is already before us that the terminology of universals makes mischief and that one way in which it makes mischief is this: It tempts us to ignore the fact that we can misapprehend what is before us. But of this more at another time.

My second comment on Price's account of thinking is this: He emphasizes the fact that in thinking we use images as well as words and he says that in using images we in some sense come nearer to instances of what we are talking about. This last point seems to me worth the most careful attention. But I cannot now give it that attention. Instead I must complain that Price in his anxiety to give images their due does on occasion, I say again on occasion, neglect a point of great importance. It is this: When we ask what happens when with the help of a symbol someone thinks of what is absent, it makes no difference to our puzzle whether the symbol is a word or an image or a picture painted on paper. Price is aware of this profoundly important point so clearly brought out by Wittgenstein, but by his very anxiety to insist that we use images he obscures it. Surely, one feels, he would not so much insist that we have images if this fact were not a help in answering the question 'What is it to attach a meaning to a symbol?' But it is not a help. It is a hindrance. It is important to recall that we have images mainly because we need to notice that they are themselves one type of symbol and that they do *not* provide an answer to the question 'What is it to attach a meaning to a symbol?' Of course we use images, and also diagrams and sketches. But this leaves untouched the questions: 'What would be the difference between a child or an adult who heard uttered the words 'tick tock" or "clock" and didn't understand the words and one who did?', 'What would be the difference between one who had an image of a clock and didn't take it as an image of a clock, and one who did?', 'What would be the difference between one who saw a clock and did not take it to be a clock and one who did?'

Price is well aware that these questions lie at the heart of the matter 'What is it to think? What is it to have an idea of things of a certain sort?' What answer does he give to this question? His whole book is his answer and as I have said one cannot summarize it. But I will attempt to give a hint of the outline of the long answer. It is on the lines of the answer given by

Wittgenstein and by Berkeley before Wittgenstein, and by others before Berkeley. Successive answers supplement and clarify each other. The outline of these answers is this:

People sometimes say that they are sure that a medicine is doing them good and even that they feel it is doing them good, but whether it is really doing them good is much more a matter of what they are able to do *after* they have taken it, than of how they feel while they are taking it. In the same way people sometimes say that they have understood what was said to them but whether they have really understood is much more a matter of how they go on after hearing the words they felt they understood than of any feelings or mental pictures they had at the time. The difference between one who did understand and one who did not understand what he saw or heard lies in this: the one had, the other had not, the power to connect what he saw or heard with other things. And whether or no a man had or had not at a certain moment the power to connect is less a matter of flashes and gleams in his mind at that moment than it is of what *subsequently* happens in his mind and his body. The most strongly charged cable is not necessarily the one that is giving off the brightest sparks, it's the one which when required drives the biggest train. The man who recognizes a wolf even in sheep's clothing is the man who is not flabbergasted but ready with an axe when the creature shows his teeth. Or, again, you exclaim, perhaps, 'A drink, a drink' and one who understands brings you a drink and not ginger ale. Or, somewhat oddly, you exclaim 'A clock' and one who understands removes the irritating thing, or brings it, or looks round and still looks round until he sees a clock or at least a sundial and having seen what looks like the right thing watches the moving hand or creeping shadow and from them looks to the sun. For Time of course is not merely the tick of a clock nor a shadow on a wall. It's the rising, setting, sun, the departure of the 8.20 and the ripening fruit. Dandelions after all do tell the time. When the child begins to connect these things he begins to know what Time is and what's a clock.

Someone unused to philosophy might feel inclined to say 'But surely we know what it is for a man or a cat to recognize a mouse when he sees it and what it is for a woman to imagine or think there is a mouse when there isn't. So what has Price done for us except explain the use of the technical phrase "aware of a universal", a phrase we could well do without since its only use is to describe incidents which are easily referred to in ordinary English?'

But this is to miss the point. Price's aim is not to teach the meaning of new words nor, of course, to teach the meaning of old ones. It is not to teach the meaning of any words, it is to bring out for us the meaning of words the meaning of which we already very well know. After all, we very well know the meanings of the words 'sane' and 'insane' and yet *upon occasion* we may find it worth while to review the meanings of these words. We know very well the meanings of the words 'kind', 'unkind', 'right', 'wrong' and yet *upon occasion* we may wish to review all the many little things that go to make an act right or wrong, kind or unkind. Price wishes to review the many little things that go to make the difference between a creature which sees a thing as a thing of a certain sort and one who sees it without seeing it as a thing of that sort, between a creature which understands pictures of, or talk about, things of a certain sort and one which does not.

It may seem academic, wrongheaded, frivolous, to embark upon so remote, so abstract, a project as that of reconsidering what is involved in the concept of having a concept. But it may turn out that this operation so academic is not so remote from life as it seems. Besides it's a free country. Every man to his taste. Some go to the dogs and some consider the concept of having the concept of Doghood, some produce music, others metaphysics, some do their job badly, others well and some very well.

As one reads Price's book one is struck by its easy yet classic elegance. It is, I find myself saying again, simple yet profound, down to earth yet far reaching, complex yet co-ordinated. Looking from this work to the classics and then back again at it one realizes that it resembles the old masters more than any mere imitation could—indeed it is an instance of the complex universal *masterly*.

XI

Paradox and Discovery

In a paper called 'Notes upon a Case of Obsessional Neurosis' first published in 1909 Freud writes:

> I shall not in the present paper attempt any discussion of the psychological significance of obsessional thinking. Such a discussion would be of extraordinary value in its results, and would do more to clarify our ideas upon the nature of the conscious and the unconscious than any study of hysteria or the phenomena of hypnosis. It would be a most desirable thing if the philosophers and psychologists who develop brilliant theoretical views upon a basis of hearsay knowledge or from their own conventional definitions would first submit to the convincing impressions which may be gained from a first hand study of the phenomena of obsessional thinking.

This passage is interesting but somewhat bewildering. If the phenomena of obsessional neurosis provide some of the most striking and typical manifestations of the unconscious then it is easy to understand that a study of these would be valuable, and even necessary, to anyone who wishes to reach correct scientific views as to the nature of the unconscious, that is, as to what goes on in the unconscious. But it is not so clear why a study of these phenomena should be valuable to one who wishes to reach a correct philosophical view as to the nature of the unconscious. For surely philosophical views about the nature of the unconscious are views as to the notion of the unconscious, that is to say views as to the logical character of statements involving the notion of the unconscious whether those statements are true or false. How can a study of what in fact happens be valuable to one who is concerned not with whether certain statements are true but with what sort of thing would have to be so if those statements were true? How can scientific enquiry be helpful to a logical, philosophical, meta-physical enquiry? And this suggests the question 'Can meta-physical enquiry ever be helpful to science?'

Take another instance. What connection is there between on the one hand enquiry as to what in fact goes on among the atoms which compose physical things and philosophical enquiry about the notion of atoms, that is enquiry about the logical peculiarities of statements about atoms, such statements as 'This grain, any grain, of polonium contains 3×10^{21} atoms.'? Enquiry as to the logical character of these statements is direc-ted towards gaining a clearer view of the procedure proper to the proof or refutation of them. Such a clearer view would enable us to remove the bewilderment that may be caused by the at least apparent conflict between statements about atoms which appear to imply that solid objects, such as crystals or stones or the chair on which one is sitting, have holes in them, and everyday statements such as 'This stone has no holes in it'. And conversely a study of the apparent conflict could lead to a clearer view of the procedure proper to the proof and refuta-tion of statements about atoms and even to a clearer view of the procedure proper to the everyday statements with which they appear to be in conflict. Scientific advance, on the other hand does nothing, can do nothing, to remove this apparent conflict.

And yet it is worth noticing that this apparent conflict does not nowadays make us distrust statements about atoms or about the electrons which the atoms contain. Indeed we are hardly conscious of any apparent conflict unless someone draws our attention to it as did Eddington when he obliged us to consider whether we should say that an apparently solid table is not solid or should say that it is solid and not made of atoms nor a swarm of electrons in motion.

Having brought this conflict before our minds Eddington made an attempt to deal with it. He suggested that the truth is that there are two tables, the commonsense table which is solid and the scientific table which is not. We are hardly sure whether to take this suggestion seriously and it certainly does not re-move our bewilderment, because we distrust the idea that the apparent conflict here arises from the fact that while the two statements 'The study table is solid', 'The study table is not solid', appear to be about the same thing, they are not. We are aware that such misunderstandings do arise. One person when he says 'The study table is sound and does not wobble' may be referring to a different table from that referred to by one who says 'The study table is not sound and it wobbles'. The one may be referring to the study table in his house, the other to the study table in his house. Of course this may happen and when it does then if a dispute arises between those who make the apparently inconsistent statements, we are quick to explain that the dispute arises from a misunderstanding by each party concerned in it as to what the other party means by the words he uses, that the dispute is not real but verbal. Again, if one person says 'The elephant is not a very large animal' and another says 'The elephant is a very large animal' the apparent conflict between these two statements may arise from the fact that while one speaker means that a particular elephant, perhaps the only one owned by a certain circus, is not very large, the other means that most elephants when fully grown are very large animals. It is true in this case that the truth or falsity of the zoologist's statement 'The elephant is a very large animal' depends upon the truth or falsity of statements as to the size of particular elephants. But this leaves it still true that the fact that a particular adult elephant is not very large is not inconsistent with the zoologist's statement. We might express this in a brief but misleading manner by saying that the zoologist is speaking about a scientific elephant or scientific animal while the other speaker is speaking about a particular, ordinary, everyday elephant, and we might say that the apparent conflict arises from a verbal misunderstanding. This situation seems rather more like that which we have to face when we consider the apparent conflict between the everyday statement, 'The study table is solid' and the scientific statement 'The study table is not solid'. Nevertheless we feel that the situations are profoundly different. This account of the conflict may be better in some ways than Eddington's but it is still profoundly wrong.

We may find it difficult to give a better account but rather than accept a bad one we may prefer to put the apparent conflict out of our minds and say perhaps that *somehow* there is no conflict, or that if there is it isn't worth bothering about. We may prefer to give our time and attention to learning more about what goes on among or within atoms rather than to a study of the logical character of statements about atoms or, more briefly, the notion of the atom. We may prefer to get on with science instead of involving ourselves in metaphysics. And this preference need not lead us into any difficulties nor make our work superficial. Such a policy may even lead to our being better placed to answer the question 'What sort of conflict, if any, is there between what scientists say about the fundamental nature of material, physical, things and our everyday statements about these things'. For by trying to establish the truth of further statements about atoms or electrons we may gain a better grasp of the procedure which establishes the truth or falsehood of such statements and of how, if at all, these statements correct those everyday beliefs about material things which do not involve the notion of atoms, still less the notion of electrons. And no doubt the same thing is true whenever we come on people who are saying what seems as though it could not be true, or could not be true unless words are being used in some new and extravagant sense. Faced with seemingly preposterous statements we are tempted to meet the situation with philosophical clamour 'It's impossible', 'It's unprovable' or 'It's only a linguistic innovation.' But it is often much better on these occasions to leave our armchairs and enter into the enquiry which has prompted serious people to say such bewildering things instead of at once demanding from these people descriptions and definitions of what it is they are doing when they speak as they do. This is still true when a scientist makes bewildering statements not now about the physical, material, world, but about the mental world. Here again no doubt it is often better to look with him at those happenings in nature which he is at least trying to describe and explain rather than involve him and ourselves in metaphysics, in attempts to describe the general character of the statements he is making. And I now feel that I ought to have realized this when I asked what now seems the foolish question 'How can a study of the phenomena of obsessional neurosis or any other phenomena of the unconscious, help to cure the bewilderment we are apt to feel when faced with statements which suggest that a man may be mistaken about his own mind?'—and, in general, 'How can scientific enquiry help to cure a logical, metaphysical, bewilderment?' After all when we come upon someone using strange instruments in a strange way, it is often better to watch him and try to imitate him and use those instruments ourselves than to ask him to describe what he is doing. Painters are often not good at describing what it is they are doing with their brushes and paints. Poets are often not good at describing what it is they are doing with words, and scientists, as we have just noticed in the case of Eddington, may make a very poor job of describing what it is they are doing. Nor can we safely turn to professional metaphysicians, to persons who specialize in describing the types of proof appropriate to various types of statement. For they often do more harm than good. Metaphysicians, amateur and professional, often make mischief. What caricatures of physics, of law, of religion, do they produce! Fortunately the professional academic metaphysician, like myself for instance, usually confines his attentions to statements so familiar to us in practice that he can't do much lasting harm. For instance, a typical metaphysician may declare that material things, that chairs and tables, can not exist, or that their existence can not be proved, or that when we speak of them we are really speaking about our own sensations. Or he tells us that the past does not exist, that time is unreal. Such assertions may shock people for a moment but they don't really cut much ice. People don't because they have been reading metaphysics come to view history with suspicion. The typical metaphysician is like one who points to some eccentricity in the character of some person or family of persons we know extremely well, and perhaps, represents this eccentricity as if it proved that the family we have so long trusted are all crazy or utterly untrustworthy or at any rate not at all what we had thought them to be. We may admit that we had not properly noticed a certain eccentricity in our friends and yet know them so well that we soon dismiss the innuendo that they are crazy, untrustworthy or pretentious. In the same way when the metaphysician speaks of some class of statements which we continually meet in everyday life we do not allow his preposterous pronouncements about them to influence our treatment of them. Here his pronouncements are ineffective rather than dangerous. It is when he speaks of statements which are rather strange to us and which themselves seem preposterous that his pronouncements more readily mislead us and may even make us mistreat those statements he professes to describe. It is here that he may make mischief. True, it is when we come upon bewildering statements that we are most apt to feel the need to call in the metaphysician, to seek professional help. But if what we want is a normal, healthy, grasp of what people are doing with words then, even when they speak strangely it is often better, as we have now said, to watch them or join with them in their work rather than to accept the well-meant ministrations of metaphysicians.

But am I now perhaps representing the metaphysician as more mischievous or more useless than he is? After all there are persons of a nervous or hypochondriacal turn of mind of whom we may say that though they do not really need a doctor they will not, and so in a sense cannot, do without him. There are people who though they have from their childhood employed with success such expressions as 'It is still in the future' or 'It is now in the past' suddenly turn upon themselves and ask 'But how can it be in the future since it doesn't yet exist?', 'How can it now be in the past since it now no longer exists?' Such idle bewilderment does not arise from any lack of practice with the expressions about which they now suddenly choose to make a fuss and no further practice with these expressions is likely to remove it. If we are to help, if we are to understand, someone who now suddenly says that nothing is in the future, nothing in the past, or that good and evil is an illusion, then we must join him in his projected enquiry, however extravagant and even pathological it may seem. And we shall always find, I believe, that it is not for nothing that these strange things are said, that there is indeed truth in them however insignificant for practice it may be and however distorted and confused is the form in which it is presented. For these strange pronouncements which purport to throw doubt upon all statements of some familiar sort, for instance statements about good and evil or statements about the past or the future, are always promoted by the speaker's having come to notice some real idiosyncrasy in the way in which all statements of the sort in question are established or refuted. A dramatist or one who writes a strange story of Lilliput or Brobdingnag may show us in human nature something which we have often encountered in everyday life and yet have not recognized, remarked. A metaphysical philosopher may show us in some species of enquiry some feature not unknown to us and yet unremarked.

If now someone asks 'Is this metaphysical enquiry, this enquiry about enquiry worth while?' we may reply 'It is worth while to those to whom it is worth while, it is worth while to those who seek to see things clearer in this remote sphere.'

What is this remote sphere and in what sense is it remote? The metaphysical philosopher asks 'How in the end can one settle questions about good and evil, about the future, about the past, about material things, about minds, about God?' The religious person or the person struggling with a moral question or the person who is asking what really happened or what is really in someone's mind, or what is happening in some machine or in some room behind a curtain, is trying to find out whether or how far a statement which is of a certain sort is true or false. The pure logician is not concerned with whether or how far a religious, moral, physical, or psychological, statement is true but with how one would know the truth of one statement of one of these types given another of the same type. The pure metaphysician goes further. He is concerned with how one could know the truth of a statement of a given type, say the moral type, not from other statements of the same type but from the sort of thing which in the end is the ground for any statement of the type in question. We might say he is concerned not with the 'domestic' logic of statements of a given type but with the ultimate logic of statements of a given type. Such a study is not ordinarily called logic but epistemology. The epistemologist, the metaphysician, traces further than does the orthodox logician the justification–refutation procedure proper to statements of a given type. But, like the pure logician, the pure metaphysician is not engaged in physical, psychological, historical, religious enquiry.

If now someone asks 'Does metaphysical enquiry serve a *practical* purpose, some purpose beyond itself? Does it in particular help or hinder those scientific, historical or other enquiries the ultimate logical character of which is the subject of metaphysics?' then the answer, as we have seen, is as follows:

(1) When a metaphysician is concerned only with statements of a sort with which we are thoroughly at home then his remarks seldom much influence our treatment of these statements whether for good or for ill. A metaphysician usually is concerned with statements of a thoroughly normal and familiar sort so that it is no wonder that metaphysical pronouncements have been more often ineffective than harmful.

(2) It may happen however that a metaphysical philosopher directs his attention upon some class of statements less familiar to us, statements which, because they are at once akin to and yet different from those we are used to, bewilder us. It is then that metaphysical comment has more influence. And this influence is, I fear, more often mischievous than beneficial. Faced with eccentric statements which already seem absurd we may readily accept either the suggestion that they are absurd or the suggestion that they imply a not merely astonishing but unbridgeable gap between appearance and reality and are as unprovable as they are irrefutable, or the more fashionable suggestion that they are not absurd and not unprovable, but are not at all what they seem.

We know that Galileo's assertions were met not merely with the words 'It isn't so' but with the *a priori* protest 'It's impossible'. Or again imagine that we are living in the early days of science and that we are faced for the first time with a scientist who says that crystals and other things which look so smooth and solid are made of small particles or atoms. How easy at this stage to reply 'But this is impossible. Our own eyes show us this isn't true. Indeed to admit that we all see what we do see and still to say that these things are not solid but are made of little things, like a heap of sand or a swarm of bees, is absurd'. For all its common sense aim this reply is metaphysical, for it contains the metaphysical assertion that what the scientist says is shown to be false by our looking for certain things and not seeing them.

Next a more cautious person may say: 'What the scientist says is not absolutely proved false by appearances. It may be true and no doubt the scientist had made certain observations which lend some probability to his hypothesis. But on the other hand his hypothesis can never be really proved—not even in the way we may prove that what looks like a clump of earth is really a swarm of bees. For no one can see even under a microscope those small particles of which the scientist speaks. His hypothesis is unprovable'. This reply too is metaphysical. Lastly there appears a more up-to-date person who says 'I think there's a misunderstanding here. The scientist is not advancing some hypothesis which in spite of all his observations remains a hypothesis. The apparent conflict with common sense arises from a failure to realize that the scientist is using old words in new ways. He is using a chess board and chess pieces to play not chess but a game of his own. What has happened is that the scientist has observed certain phenomena and now wants a notation in which to present them. We need not grudge him the use of words which we commonly use in more workaday contexts. If we lend them to him we need not put in a condition that he must use them more or less as we do. On the contrary if we put in any condition it should be that he makes it clear that he is not using them in the usual way. In any case it is too late to make conditions now. The scientist has taken our words and uses them, not to make absurd statements, nor to advance unverifiable hypotheses but simply to name the phenomena he has observed'.

Each of these accounts of the logical character of statements about invisible particles seems to me to distort their character, but, fortunately, in this case these accounts now do little practical harm. For they make little or no difference to the practice of those who make and consider such statements in the course of physical enquiry. Some of us know little of science but then we don't make these statements nor investigate their truth. And scientists who do make them know their character too well in practice to allow metaphysical gossip to influence their treatment of them. The Somersetshire Smith-Jones may be rather an eccentric branch of the family but if we know them well we are no more put off by a lot of talk about them than we are put off by the derogatory and really outrageous comments which some wrong-headed people permit themselves to make about even the most conventional of the Smith-Jones. And those of us who have not the pleasure of knowing the Somersetshire branch of the family regard with suspicion any innuendo that they are not all they pretend to be. For we know that they are regarded with profound respect by those who know them best and we ourselves come every day upon many benefits conferred upon the community by these innocent, these invaluable, eccentrics. This surely is how those of us who have not the advantage of knowing physics feel about all those strange statements with which physicists are so much at home. We are convinced that however bizarre the forms and procedures of physics they nevertheless provide a knowledge of nature wider and more profound than our own. And as for physicists themselves it is only in their idle moments that they are disturbed by the comments of metaphysicians on the side lines. The course of their enquiries remains unaffected.

But we must not forget that things were not always so even in physics. The struggle against the *a priori* attitude has been a long one. As to whether it ever happens nowadays that even in physics this attitude plays a part in the opposition to a new theory which calls not merely for a revision in our ideas as to what is so but for some modification of our ideas themselves, I cannot say. Physicists are well aware that a calculus which has served us well may need to be modified and the habit of open-minded enquiry is strong in them. On the other hand the habit of rejecting too quickly what smells of contradiction, especially when it is tiresome, dies hard. And the empirical attitude itself may make one too impatient of statements eccentrically related to observation. Some cosmologists, I believe, have not long ago suggested that matter is always and everywhere coming into being even in what has appeared to be empty space. Have they on any occasion found the difficulties of presenting the case for their theory increased by a tendency to meet it too abruptly, if not with the words 'It cannot be true', still with the words 'It's chronically speculative, it could not be proved' or 'It's only a new way of describing well known phenomena'. Let us hope that the answer is 'No, nowadays nothing approaching such a reaction is ever met in physics. Of course physicists preserve a properly critical attitude and they do not expect perfection of each other and are on their guard against contradiction and against bogus theories which purport to do much and do nothing. But nowadays no theory is resisted, still less rejected because it involves not merely revising our beliefs as to what is actual but our conceptions of what is conceivable'.

Even if we may hope that in the sphere of physics it never happens that the enquiry called for by eccentric statements is hindered or distorted by an inadequate grasp of their nature, we cannot pretend that this never happens in other spheres. One might have expected that in the sphere of religion everyone would have learned by now to move carefully and neither at once to accept nor hastily to reject what sounds bewildering. But no, even here we still find a tendency to reject strange statements with impatience, to turn from them as absurd or unprovable or to write them down as metaphor—deceptive or at best merely picturesque. Only a few months ago someone came to me troubled about the old but bewildering statement that Christ was both God and man. He had asked those who taught him theology how this *could* be true. Their answers had not satisfied him. I was not able to tell him what the doctrine means. But I did remind him that though some statements which seem self-contradictory are self-contradictory others are not, that indeed some of the most preposterous statements ever made have turned out to convey the most tremendous discoveries.

I know we all know this but I submit that we sometimes don't have it in mind when we need it. *One* cause for this is a very proper fear of being taken in by the bogus, or a very proper dread of confusion. But after all the proper way of ascertaining whether one who makes a confusing statement is confused is to try to come at what sort of things would make for this statement and what would make against it. For instance we may ask one who says that 'Christ was one with God' how this statement is connected with what Christ is reported to have said, namely 'Neither pray I for these alone, but for them also which shall believe on me through their word; that they all may be one; as Thou, Father, art in me, and I in Thee, that they also may be one in us'. We may then consider what it is about human beings which is referred to by one who says that they are not one with God but could become so and in what way it is alleged that Christ was different so that He was one with God and how this is consistent with those despairing words 'My God, my God, why hast Thou forsaken me'? I am not saying that *whenever* we are faced with an eccentric, boundary-breaking or near boundary-breaking statement, we reject it and refuse to give it the attention it deserves or treat it as if it were what it is not. Faced with such a statement we do not *always* say 'It can't be true', 'It can't be proved' or 'It is merely a metaphorical description for admitted facts recently discovered or long known'. Of course not. We are upon the whole well aware not only that language is flexible but also that its purpose is not merely to report facts briefly and sometimes to raise emotion or promote a policy. But I am claiming that sometimes when an extravagant statement is made we become bewildered, annoyed, or alarmed and mishandle the situation, especially when we cannot say that the speaker is joking and also cannot call him a poet, but must call him a scientist, a mathematician, or a philosopher. The speaker himself may insist that he is speaking absolutely literally and not with licence. The reasons he offers for his statement may be most conventional. We cannot deny that that which he says is of a certain sort has indeed a whole assembly of the characteristic features of things of that sort. It's only that it lacks some and that the lack of these seems fatal to his claims. Hasn't he over-looked this? No he has not. That's what beats us. Even then we sometimes grasp the situation. Probably no one made any bother when someone first called a toy dog a dog or a locomotive an iron horse. I cannot here set out the factors which make for and against our grasping the general character of what is being done by one who makes a paradoxical statement perhaps openly, perhaps with all the air of doing no such thing. But one factor is this: we are the more apt to fail to grasp what is being done the more the reasons for the statement made are so overwhelming that we can hardly call it a metaphor or a paradox while yet the reasons against it are so overwhelming that it seems preposterous to say that it is literally true. The affinity it unfolds is so profound that we cannot but take it seriously and yet the difference it ignores is so enormous as to seem to take from the words of the statement not merely some of their usual sense but all of it and even to render the statement no longer of the family to which it purports to belong. For instance as we have noticed when someone first says to us that when to an observer best placed to see it a table looks solid and not an agitated swarm of particles it may yet not be solid and be a swarm of particles we may be suspicious of this statement. If the table we sit at, the floor we stand on, is a swarm of particles there seems nothing solid to go on. The prestige of physics prevents our taking this suspicion seriously or expressing it openly. But the suspicion, the confusion, is then covered rather than cured. And if now we meet someone who says that even when a person to himself seems calm and not agitated he may yet be agitated and not calm we may again be suspicious. We may feel that one who thus suggests that a person may mistakenly think that he is not angry or not pleased, that even here appearances may be deceptive to one best placed to know, is taking from words, not merely something of their usual sense, but just that which makes them words about the mind and not about some external object open on the same terms to the observation of anyone. Once more we feel ourselves on the way to absurdity or if not, to a hypothesis which can never be verified or to a hypothesis which could not be refuted and thus tells us nothing or to a metaphor which really tells us only what we already knew.

In such situations at once so serious and so absurd we sometimes permit our bewilderment to stop, to weaken or distort enquiry. We say 'But this can show us nothing, this can explain nothing' and thus half deny ourselves that view of the actual, that power to place on the manifold of nature those phenomena which seemed anomalous, which a changing conception may give us.

To sum up what we have said so far as to the value of metaphysics: Metaphysicians draw attention, though often in a confused way, to some imperfectly recognized features of the procedure characteristic of a class of statements or questions. When the statements with which a metaphysician is concerned are thoroughly familiar to us what he says has little effect on our practice.

But when the statements with which he is concerned are eccentric and we are not quite at home with them his words sometimes have more effect and when they do this effect is often unfortunate.

One way to meet the danger of metaphysics, whether it is proclaimed by professionals or muttered by oneself to oneself, is to pay no attention to it and find out in practice the character of the statements that puzzle us.

This is an excellent plan. It has, however, two defects. First, even in one who follows it, it may leave a lingering bewilderment and even some suspicion. Second, in adopting this plan one may be leaving to their fate those whose bewilderment or suspicion, or despair of real proof, or feeling that it's all a matter of words, makes them unable or unwilling to give to strange, to revolutionary statements, the attention they require and deserve. In short sometimes one feels a need for more and better metaphysics if it can be had. And if it can then surely it may be used to supplement the prescription: Find the proof of the pudding in the eating.

Metaphysical theories have at least this merit: they combat each other. And this conflict so far from preventing progress promotes it. The dialectic moves tortuously on. And though, as we noticed, progress towards metaphysical apprehension may have little practical effect, and may have bad effects, it may have good effects.

But now when and how does metaphysics have a good practical effect? (1) Consider first armchair statements which are not metaphysical and have a good effect. Pure mathematics and pure logic are concerned with what statements are inconsistent with others, with what statements logically imply others, and not with whether those statements are true. This is what gives the principles of logic and mathematics that feature so characteristic of them—they are correct no matter what happens, they would be correct no matter what were to happen. And yet pure mathematics and even pure logic is not useless to us in science and in everyday life when we are trying to grasp what in fact is so.

It may suddenly strike us as a mystery that principles which are correct, no matter what happens, should yet help us when we are concerned with what happens. But we know they do. How do they? They are, of course, helpless by themselves to tell us anything as to what, though it might not have been, in fact is so. They are no substitute for our eyes and ears. But when we are trying to grasp a mass of data provided by observation and experience we may murmur to ourselves the purest principles such as '3786 less 587 is 3199'. And though murmuring this by itself tells us nothing as to how much profit a trader has made in a year or how many sheep we now have after the disastrous floods, it may help us to extract from the bewildering mass of detail which observation has presented to us that aspect of the situation which now concerns us. But I should like to be clearer still about how this happens. Another instance may help. Suppose I am told that my friend Alfred is now to receive an income of £780 a year. I know quite well what this means but for a moment I may hardly take it in, especially if my own income and that of the people I know is usually described in terms of shillings or pounds a week. I may say to myself '£780 a year. Let's see, that's £15 a week—that's as good or better than I can ever hope to get'. I may say this although it's a logical impossibility that a man should receive £780 a year without getting £15 a week and vice versa. I do so because although every investigation and every comparison relevant to the one statement is equally relevant to the other, the one in terms of so much a week brings to my mind the situation it describes in a thousand and one comparisons which the other implies but leaves latent. Again one may look at a cube or even say 'It's a cube' without realizing that it has twelve edges until someone murmurs 'A cube must have twelve edges, like a matchbox not like a pyramid'.

Again suppose someone says 'Today is Sunday. Well it happened here five days ago on a Thursday'. You may say that's impossible, logically impossible, and so combat a confused account of what is so and thus leave the way open for a better account.

(2) But now to recall how mathematical or logical armchair truth may help one's apprehension of what in fact is so is not to show how metaphysics may do this. Far from it. For the more clearly one sees how a mathematical truth may do this the more clearly one sees that metaphysics does not in the same way do so. Does it do so in some other way? And if so how?

Take an instance:

Told that a man left London at 10 one morning and reached New York at 10 minutes to 10 that same morning we might easily at one time have rejected such a story as impossible. This did not matter while we were not concerned with people or things which travel very fast. But the moment we do become concerned with such things we find ourselves at a loss for a word and at the same time find ourselves at a loss in our efforts to place on the manifold of the possible and the actual the events which at first surprise us. In our efforts to do so we find in our mouths bewildering words such as 'Left at 10 and arrived at 10 to 10'. It will not do to say that this is impossible, that this statement is internally inconsistent, that one who makes this statement is making a logical blunder like one who says 'Today is Sunday. Well it happened here five days ago on Thursday'. On the other hand it will not do to say that one who says 'It is impossible that a man should leave London at 10 one morning and arrive in New York at 10 to 10' is just ignorant of how fast one can travel. If we tell him about this he may be astonished, he may even for a moment be inclined to agree that a man may nowadays leave London at 10 and arrive in New York at 10 to 10. But in the next moment he may say 'No, however fast a man travels it is a logical impossibility that he should leave London at 10 and arrive in New York at 10 to 10'. And in saying this he too does not make a logical error like one who says 'It is impossible that today being Sunday the ceremony took place nine days ago on a Friday' or like one who says 'Whatever happens it is impossible that without deceiving anyone a man should lie', forgetting that a lie may be a failure.

'But' it may be said 'surely all this can be explained and explained quite easily. It's all a matter of words. Surely what is meant by saying that a man left London at 10 and arrived in New York at 10 to 10 is simply that when he left London the clocks then pointed to 10 o'clock and when he reached New York the clocks then pointed to 10 to 10'. But this is not what is meant. For this would have been true had someone left London when the clocks then pointed to 10 to 10 travelled in a slow sailing ship and arrived at New York to find the clocks there pointing to 10 to 10 because the clocks there had been very slow when he started or because someone there had put them all back or because the clocks there went very, very slowly.

'But' it may be said 'what is meant is that clocks in London may be pointing to the right time, 10 o'clock, when the traveller starts and that clocks in New York which are right may be pointing to 10 to 10 when he arrives there.'

But this is not an explanation. How does this differ from what was originally said, namely that a man may leave London at 10 and reach New York at 10 to 10?

'Look here' it may be said 'the right time at any place is something which is known from the position of the sun in the sky at that place. Now when the traveller left London the sun was in that position from which it could be inferred that the time there was 10 o'clock; when he reached New York the sun was in a position which made the time there 10 to 10.'

Gradually the position is becoming clearer. But notice (1) that this greater clarity has been achieved by considering not how one statement about the time at which something happened can be inferred from another but by calling to mind how such statements are known *in the end*, that is not from other statements of the same sort but from observation and comparison. In other words it has been accomplished *not* by examining what one might call the ordinary *domestic* logic of statements as to the time at which some event takes place but their *fundamental* logic, that is their metaphysical character.

Notice (2) that though the position is now clearer it is still far from clear. Indeed one might say that the heart of the difficulty is still untouched. For in the explanation there occurs the expression 'the right time at a particular place' or 'the time at a particular place'. How can the time at one place be different from what it is at another? No doubt this question evinces confusion. This confusion *may* be removed by simply continuing to use such expressions and thus showing their value and their meaning. But it may also be met by *describing* how they are used. Further when it is said that from the position of the sun we may *infer* the time and thus know the time at which a traveller departs does this mean (a) that from the position of the sun we may safely infer the time, as we may infer the time from a usually very reliable clock, or does it mean (b) that the sun is in a special position in that it *could* not be wrong because when we speak of the time, the right time, the real time, we mean the position of the sun? If (b) is meant is (b) true? *Is* it a logical impossibility that the sun should stand still for a time as it is said to have done on an occasion when the Israelites were fighting the Amorites (Joshua x. 12)? Put the matter another way: If everything appears to go on normally except that the sun appears not to move or only very slowly ought we to say not that the sun has slowed down but that everything else has happened much faster than usual? Hardly. And yet, if not, then answer (b) above is false and it is not only the sun which tells us the time. But now if we give the answer (a) above then what besides the sun is relevant to what time it is? There is again no doubt that these difficulties can be removed. Again it is true that they *may* be removed by merely continuing to use the words which occasion them and thus making plain to anyone who is ready to go with us the value and the meaning of such words. But again it is possible to supplement this 'the proof of the pudding is in the eating' method.

We may supplement a procedure in which by using certain verbal instruments we *show* their use by an *explanation* of their use. And it is worth noticing that without this explanation some people may refuse to go with us. They may refuse to start at all. They may take advantage of the apparent absurdity of such statements as 'He left London at 10 and reached New York at 10 to 10' to turn away from such statements with the excuse 'It's impossible' and thus take from us all opportunity to show their use. Or more subtle people may avoid the impact of these statements by saying 'These statements don't mean what they appear to mean'. It is worth noticing also that even someone who learns to use the most surprising statements about the timing of events, including perhaps the statement that events simultaneous with respect to one observer need not be simultaneous with respect to another, may yet have in his mind a lurking bewilderment which he hardly likes to mention even to himself, which he might indeed deny, which might never show itself plainly except in the confusedness of the explanation he offers when he tries to explain what is meant by such statements to one who is on the point of paying no proper attention to them on the ground that they could not be true. In other words even when we have come to be able to make statements which at first seemed absurd we may yet on occasion fall back into bewilderment especially if our early difficulty has never been adequately faced. Such a resurgence of a difficulty we once felt but perhaps never expressed may call for the most careful and subtle analysis.

Such difficulty, it is worth noticing, may have a source

which is not purely intellectual and yet is still intimately connected with an intellectual source. Paradoxical statements are apt to annoy and alarm us and this may happen not because they make us recognize what we would rather not but because they involve a departure from the very habits which secure us against confusion. While in all we say we follow faithfully normal practice or even a practice more rigid than the normal, we are safe we feel from folly and unreason. The moment the bonds of convention are broken we begin to fear that words are losing their meanings, that, flouting logic, we are losing the light of reason and drifting from freedom to licence, and from licence to confusion with madness as an unmentioned limit.

Such fear, such obsessional fear, of any concept which begins to be not quite itself may indeed join with inadequate comprehension of such eccentricity to cramp our power to conceive the conceivable. For it is with words mainly that we delineate the conceivable and if we never allow words to be a little eccentric, never allow ourselves to apply a word to any state of affairs actual or conceivable, to which it would not customarily be applied, we are without means to refer to any state of affairs for which there is not yet a word, any possibility undreamt of in our philosophy.

But all this leaves it still true that amongst the measures we may usefully take against nervous and precipitate rejection or denigration of seemingly absurd statements is an explicit explanation of how the seeming contradiction is not a contradiction—a metaphysical explanation of this.

And there is another factor which may on such occasions make metaphysical enquiry worth while. For metaphysical enquiry may be valuable not only because it removes improper grounds for suspicion but also because it brings out proper grounds for suspicion. For though a general suspicion of any statement which breaks or stretches the bonds of conventional usage, is far too sweeping, it is not altogether without foundation. And a particular suspicion about a particular statement of this sort, though it may be exaggerated, and may even be entirely misplaced, is often not entirely misplaced. An instance will show the need for both an almost obsessional suspicion of paradoxical, crazy sounding statements and also the need to prevent this suspicion itself going crazy—the old double need for tradition and for freedom. Not many years ago suspicion of the old paradoxical statements of metaphysical philosophy reached at once a new justification and a new intensity. A careful consideration of such old paradoxes as 'Knowledge of the minds of others is impossible', 'Knowledge of the past is impossible', 'Knowledge of good and evil is impossible', led to the suspicion that these old sceptical doctrines are senseless. The doctrine that these paradoxical doctrines are senseless was however itself paradoxical and aroused suspicion. This suspicion led to a further examination of the old sceptical pronouncements and this further examination showed that they are senseless only when taken at their face value and are not senseless when taken as misleading ways of bringing out idiosyncrasies in the way in which statements about the minds of others, about the past, about good and evil, are in the end known.

The careful comparison of the strange statements of metaphysics, with other, with more normal statements, the explicit study of their character, in short the metaphysics of metaphysics, gave us in the end a better grasp of their nature than had years of practice with them, and what is more, it enabled us to work with them much better, to extract from the confusion in them the truth. In other words: our blustering and yet hesitant treatment of the puzzling statements of metaphysics had brought us to a point at which we wondered whether they had any character at all, good or bad. But some careful consideration of them, in short the metaphysics of metaphysics, enabled us to see them as neither more nor less than what they are, and at the same time to find the good, the truth, in them.

And the metaphysics of metaphysics is a parable which carries us beyond itself. It suggests how with other puzzling statements which are not metaphysical a few words about their character, the metaphysics of their nature, though dangerous, since it may so readily mislead, may be helpful.

But how is this metaphysics to be done, how is this better understanding reached? When we come on anything strange and bewildering we compare it with something we know. Some primitive people, I am told, call a telephone message a 'message on poles' and a wireless message 'a message on poles without the poles'. A scientist may call electricity a current and light a wave. In showing us how the strange is not so strange, he speaks strangely. And if the scientist is now himself a puzzle to us and his statements bewilder us, we may remember other statements like his but less puzzling. For we can remember how people speak of currents of air although no one sees the wind but only trees bent like weeds in a stream, leaves drifting and sinking. Indeed we are not at all unfamiliar with strange statements. We sometimes say 'She has her mother's face'.

In general both the bewilderment in the mind of one who rejects a class of paradoxical statements and the latent be-wilderment which may persist even in the mind of one who comes to accept them, may be met by a careful comparison of the mode of coming at the truth or falsehood of these eccentric statements with the mode of coming at the truth or falsehood of (a) the more normal members of the family to which they belong and of (b) other eccentric statements in other families. For instance, bewilderment about certain seemingly preposterous statements about the simultaneity and dates of events may be cured by a careful review of what is offered in proof or disproof of these abnormal statements and careful noting of how this is like and of how it is different from what is offered in proof or disproof of the most normal satements about the simultaneity and dates of events. In the end we may gain not merely a better understanding of the abnormal in the light of the normal but also in the light of the abnormal a better understanding of the normal, the normal we had thought we understood so well. Before Einstein we thought we had an excellent grasp of the procedure proper to the proof and dis-proof of statements as to the dates and places at which events occur. So we had, but not a perfect grasp. Our apprehension of the difference between 'They happened at the same mo-ment' and 'They happened when our clock struck five, when the shadow of the church reached the trees' was imperfect. Our apprehension of the difference between 'They both hap-pened at the same place' and 'They both happened under the same stars' was imperfect. Our apprehension of the relation between the verification of statements as to time and statements as to place was imperfect. The imperfection of our apprehen-sion of the mode of verification proper to these statements for a long time caused no trouble. And Berkeley's was a voice calling in the wilderness. Later it did cause trouble, later we had to reconsider how it is that we do settle questions as to the dates and places of events and in doing so we won a better grasp of that procedure. In general when we come upon words, statements, thoughts, which bewilder us and still seem as though they are true then, just as when we come upon anything else which bewilders us, we may meet this bewilderment by the comparison of kind with kind, and in the end of case with case.

But this very procedure of putting one thing beside another which is so valuable to us, so necessary to our understanding, also misleads us. Each sunset would be another miracle if we did not see it in the light of so many other occasions, including, of course, not only those involving the earth and the sun, but also all those which, whatever their variety, involve a spinning sphere and a source of light. A stranger may put us in mind of someone else and so seem very understandable, and when someone acts strangely we may try to understand this by recalling what he used to be. But though the past may shed a light upon the present it may also obscure it. It is sometimes a mistake to call someone by the name they called him as a child. Sylvia as Mr. Garnett showed us in his story *Lady into Fox* may become no longer Sylvia. In every name there is this danger. The murderers of Banquo were, as they insisted, men. But then, as Macbeth remarked, 'hounds, and greyhounds, mongrels, spaniels, curs, shoughs, water-rugs, and demi-wolves, are clept all by the name of dogs'. We call this jealousy and also that, call that love and also this; and sometimes in thus marking an affinity we miss a difference.

Nor does the setting of one thing beside another work against understanding only by making too little of a difference. It may make too much of it as when we say of someone 'He is not to be trusted' and half forget how little any of us can be. It may at once make too much of it and too little. People have sometimes turned from music or painting that is new to them with the words 'It's not really music', 'It's not really art'. On such occasions they do indeed mark a difference between the new they reject and the old they accept. But at the same time it does not occur to them that the new may differ from the old not only in

K

that it does not achieve what the old achieved but also in this, that it does not aim at just what the old attempted. They thus represent a difference as a failure. Even when this is pointed out they may still insist that this is not music or not what they call music. 'It may have certain similarities' they say 'but it's different'. And, saying this, they may deny themselves that apprehension of what they reject which they might have if they could view it not less in the light of what they accept but more freely.

Metaphysical philosophers do the same when they suddenly insist that what has been counted knowledge is not, that some kind of reasoning which has been counted rational is not really rational. They too represent a difference as a failure. For instance those who declare that our knowledge of the external world is not really knowledge reach this result by comparing it, contrasting it with other knowledge, especially with knowledge of how things appear. And those philosophers who say that when scientists and the rest of us reason from present observation and past experience to confidence as to what has not yet been observed this reasoning isn't really rational, reach their result by comparing, contrasting, this reasoning with other reasoning. Asked the reason for their extraordinary pronouncement they point to the difference between, for instance, a doctor who, in the light of a patient's symptoms, says 'Gastric ulcer' and an accountant who, in the light of a man's liabilities and assets, says 'Bankrupt', or one who, informed that both of two babies were born last week, says that the chance that they were born on the same day is 7 in 49. The difference which philosophers remark here is here indeed: the doctor's conclusion ventures more than his premisses. But those who mark the difference between those who venture and those who do not by calling the former irrational show themselves forgetful of another difference, namely this: those who, like the doctor, draw a conclusion which calls for confirmation beyond their premisses are not pretending not to do so, they are not arriving at the security of the cautious. Those who call the doctor, the prophet, the tipster and the scientist, irrational as opposed to one who only records, reports, calculates and describes, recognize the difference in achievement but not the difference in the art.

They are in this respect like those who say of an explanation which does not go beyond the facts to be explained that it is not really an explanation.

We do the same sort of thing when, faced with some seemingly preposterous statement such as 'This table is a swarm of particles', we call it 'absurd', or 'chronically unverifiable', or 'a verbal innovation'.

In instance after instance the very procedure of setting one thing beside another so necessary to our understanding of anything also creates misunderstanding.

How are we to meet this difficulty? What is the difference between the comparison, the reflection, which helps our apprehension of things and that which hinders it?

We all know the person who when he goes abroad looks sharply about him but remarks only how this is just like what we have at home or not like what we have at home. His outlook, we may say, is insular, procrustean. We have met him in ourselves. For on foreign tours one sometimes feels tired, cross, old. The so-called policemen are ridiculous, the people who push so lack self control and manners, the tea we at last obtain is hardly tea. Perhaps in the morning, after sleep, we see things differently as we sit drinking coffee in sunshine which is surprisingly brilliant but not too bright.

Sometimes when a child sees something for the first time and we, wishing to help him understand, tell him what it is, he hardly seems to hear us. Perhaps he is at a play for the first time, a play about a sleeping beauty awakened by a prince's kiss, or a fairy queen enamoured of an ass. The child watches without a word. We have a word for it. We say perhaps, 'It's a fairy story; it's not something that really happens.' But the child still silently watches with the intentness of a lover or an enemy, only without their preconceptions. Perhaps this is part of why we are told that if we wish to find the truth, we must become as little children.

This is all very well, but after all, one who understands was not born yesterday. He is a person with experience and one who sees things now in the light of that experience. The trouble is that the concepts, without which we do not connect one thing with another, are apt to become a network which confines our minds. We need to be at once like someone who has seen much and forgotten nothing, and also like one who is seeing everything for the first time.

It is, I believe, extremely difficult to breed lions. But there was at one time at the Dublin zoo a keeper by the name of Mr. Flood who bred many lion cubs without losing one. Asked the secret of his success, Mr. Flood replied, 'Understanding lions'. Asked in what consists the understanding of lions, he replied, 'Every lion is different'. It is not to be thought that Mr. Flood, in seeking to understand an individual lion, did not bring to bear his great experience with other lions. Only he remained free to see each lion for itself.

XII

Tolerance

I would rather express the question I am asking in the old form 'What is tolerance?' than in the 'verbal' form 'What is meant by the word "tolerance"?' For the verbal form obscures the identity between what I here attempt to do and that which may be attempted by one who neither uses nor mentions the word 'tolerance' but speaks entirely in Chinese, Russian or Greek. Questions of the sort 'What is tolerance?' have an embarrassing feature which was remarked long ago when Socrates used to ask 'What is justice?,' 'What is virtue?,' 'What is knowledge?' However solemn the face one puts on when one asks such questions a mocking voice is apt to reply 'But don't you know? Don't we all know?' It is true that he who says 'But don't we all know?' may, when we ask him 'Well, and what is justice?' or 'What then is tolerance?,' have little to say in reply. But does this prove that he doesn't know, that we don't know what these familiar things are? It does not. It isn't true that those who can talk more about a thing always know more about it whether it be religion or love or justice or tolerance.

On the other hand, words, even when they are about things very familiar to us, sometimes remind us of something in them we have come to neglect and, what is more, sometimes show us something in them we have never remarked. Hate and love we knew before Plato, Flaubert or Proust wrote about them. Nevertheless, these men and others have given us a greater apprehension of the varieties of hatred and of love, of their entanglement with each other, and of their relations with honesty, honour, degradation, war and peace.

I am not a novelist or a poet and I can not present in a problem-play the problems of tolerance. Confined as I am by habit and circumstance to general terms, what can I say about tolerance which isn't already not only known but well recognized? Little or nothing.

Tolerance has been much praised and we easily call to mind the sorts of situation in which tolerance is good and intolerance bad. We may forget how false tolerance may be. A man may meet the intolerable behaviour of another with tolerant words and tolerant actions while there is in his heart a bitter resentment, which he conceals, perhaps from a regard for his own profit or the welfare of his family or the welfare of the state, or perhaps because he thinks he ought to be tolerant. More deceptive still, a man may conceal not only from others but also from himself the inward intolerance that lies behind his outward tolerance.

These falsehoods which may lurk in tolerance are part of the reasons why the soft answer which 'turneth away wrath' so often does the opposite. People suspect tolerance; sometimes wrongly but often rightly. For it's those who aim high who are most readily hypocrites, and in this those who aim at tolerance are no exception.

Tolerance whether false or genuine may be foolish. We may remember the words 'whosoever shall smite thee on the right cheek, turn to him the other also' without forgetting that one outrage may lead to another and a second to a third— a third of such a kind that whether or not we *ought* to tolerate it we *shall* not. A man who aims to be tolerant should envisage the limits of his own tolerance.

And tolerance, even when it is genuine and not likely to lead to something which the tolerant man himself will not stand, may be hurtful to others. A host may tolerate the rudeness of a guest and do so not only at his own expense but at the expense of his other guests. Tolstoy at one time forbore to punish the peasants who cheated him. Whether he acted wrongly or rightly this tolerance involved his children and his wife. A nation may be prepared to accept the overbearing, even the violent, actions of another. I am not now concerned to say anything as to when such tolerance is right and when it is wrong, but only to point out what is obvious, namely, that such tolerance may involve other nations, other people, men, women, and children.

There is also a tolerance which, rightly or wrongly, people dislike, not because they suspect it isn't genuine, not because they think it will lead to further outrage, not because they think it shows too little regard for others, but because they think it shows that he who is being tolerant shows too little regard for himself. People say 'A man should stand up for himself.' Alexy Alexandrovitch in Tolstoy's *Anna Karenina* felt society contemptuous of him because he did not take more vigorous action against his wife and Vronsky. On the other hand, there are those who insist that we should be tolerant not seven times but seventy times seven. But even among those who set very high the limits of proper tolerance few will deny that there are limits; nearly all will allow that some insults, some injuries to oneself, call for some measure of resistance, even violent measures.

But now that we have recalled those occasions when tolerance is false, or foolish, or unfair to others or unfair to oneself, we may remember those who have urged that a certain inward tolerance is, even in extreme cases, not out of place. Christ on the cross said 'Father forgive them for they know not what they do,' and I think He would have included amongst those He prayed for not only the soldiers of whom we might say 'They knew no better' but also Pilate, the chief priests and Judas, who 'ought to have known better.' We do not regard Christ's tolerance as false or out of place. We do not think that it was achieved at the price of deceiving Himself about human beings. On the contrary, we feel He knew their hypocrisy, their treachery, their cowardice and their cruelty and yet could still see them as worth saving, still care for them. He knew that Peter would deny Him but then, in the man who lacked the courage to stand by Him, He saw also the man who would later die for what He believed to be the truth.

Christ's tolerance was not the unloving tolerance of one who with a half-mocking smile looks on human beings as ridiculous puppets, nor even that of one who sadly and hopelessly looks on them as madmen forever playing a crazy play. In Christ there was, for all His knowledge of human beings, still a love of them, and a hope that many, a confidence that some, would achieve what He called 'eternal life'.

Some who have tried to show us a way of life have seemed

to say that life can be won only by overcoming 'the will to live,' only by overcoming those desires for something for oneself which often lead to intolerance, to destruction, and in the end to disappointment.

But in this doctrine there lurks a subtle falsehood which can take tolerance to a perfection, which, like many other perfections, destroys itself. For in so far as a man wins tolerance —even an understanding tolerance that has within it still a love or care for others—at the price of coming to care for nothing for himself, he loses the power to share the desires of those who still for themselves love music, pictures, wine, cars and horses. Tolerance which is bought at such a price leaves a man unable to take life for himself and harms his power to give life to others. For however cleverly a tolerant and kindly father conceals the fact that he is playing trains with his children entirely for their sake, he won't give the pleasure he could have given had there been in him still a love of locomotives, even toy locomotives.

There are then forms of tolerance at which men look askance. Even genuine, just, understanding, loving tolerance is not enough. This leaves it still true that we need it. This leaves it no less true that without it we may find that time for us is over before it is regained, that death has come for us before we have found life.

As this conference on tolerance and intolerance draws to an end, one may find oneself asking 'What good has there been in it?' We have met together and spoken with each other about these things and have thereby done something to show each other and perhaps a few people who hear of our conference our concern about intolerance and tolerance. But have we from our talks and discussions learned anything? We have asked 'What is tolerance?' and 'What are the limits of tolerance?' or 'What is right and proper tolerance?' But have we for all our words been able to say anything we didn't know already? I feel some embarrassment about this.

Perhaps we would have done better to ask 'What are the causes of intolerance and of tolerance?' Then we might have learned something from those who have studied the hidden mechanisms of the mind. However, in fact we asked 'What is tolerance?' and 'What is right and proper tolerance?' and 'What are the principles in accordance with which one can decide in any particular case whether one ought or ought not to tolerate what other people are doing?' It is not surprising that answers to these questions tend to be platitudinous when they are not false. For we know what tolerance is as we know what justice, honesty, poetry, argument and gambling are. Consequently any answer to the question 'What is tolerance?' will, unless it's false, tell us only what in a sense we knew already. In general, when the kind of thing with regard to which someone asks 'What is it for a thing to be of that kind' is familiar to him, any correct answer will be platitudinous, unless it sets in a new light what he knew before.

Sometimes an answer which does this is achieved. For instance, before Aristotle or any other logician spoke we knew what it is to argue, to reason, to reason badly and to reason well. Nevertheless, Aristotle showed us at least certain varieties of reasoning in orderly array, in a light in which we had not seen them before. And his successors have continued this work. Even a simple statement such as, 'a cube is a solid contained by squares and a square is an equal-sided rectangle' may make us grasp the relations between cubes and squares and other things as we had not grasped them before.

In such cases the need expressed by one who asks a question of the sort 'What is it for a thing to be of this kind?'—for instance a cube, or a syllogism—is met by setting out the conditions which are severally necessary and together sufficient for a thing to be of that kind; it is met by presenting a definition.

Unfortunately the success of this procedure of definition may encourage a habit of thinking that the need expressed by a 'What is . . . ?' question is always met when a definition can be provided and may also encourage the more obstinate habit of thinking that such a need cannot be met in any other way, cannot be met except by a definition.

It is easy to recall occasions when a definition does not meet a need. If someone who knows what poetry is nevertheless asks 'What is poetry?' he is not likely to be satisfied with the answer 'Poetry is the art of writing poems and a poem is a metrical composition, especially of an elevated character.' And if someone asks 'What is a woman?' it is safe to bet that he won't be satisfied by the answer 'A woman is an adult, female, human being.'

The more obstinate habit of thought is that of thinking that when someone asks 'What is poetry?' or 'What is honesty?' or 'What is love?' or 'What is tolerance?' his need cannot be met unless, is not met until, a definition is provided. And yet it is easy to see that this idea too is mistaken. Stendhal writes on love. In his *De L'Amour* he sets out certain varieties of love and mentions typical features of each. He does not pretend to give a correct definition of love and its varieties as a logician gives a definition of syllogistic reasoning and of the varieties of syllogism. But what he writes is not useless. On the contrary, it does much to bring in order before the mind the many forms of love and their relations to what is not love.

And what Stendhal does in *De L'Amour* is taken further in his novels; although these, of course, are still further from any attempt to bring before the mind the nature and varieties of love by giving definitions and principles. An artist, who by writing a story about real or imaginary happenings, shows us something in the familiar, does so not by propounding principles but by presenting particular things, people, happenings in such a way as to throw light on them, and thus on an infinity of others. One who has long possessed a vast but disorderly collection of real or artificial flowers or butterflies may be astonished when a child who is dumb, without a word arranges these familiar possessions in such a way that each and all of them can now be seen as they had not been seen before.

We know all this; and yet there lurks in us, especially in those whose trade is to talk, a tendency to fear that we have no proper grasp of what it is for a thing to be of a certain kind unless, until, we can define what it is for a thing to be of that kind, until we can set out foolproof rules by which one may decide whether a thing is of that kind or not. And this fear may lead us either to pretend that we have less grasp of a concept than we have or to pretend that we have foolproof rules for its application when we have not.

These considerations apply when we ask not 'What is tolerance?' but 'What is proper tolerance?' This question, it is true, is a moral question, and in the case of a moral question as opposed to a purely conceptual question as to what it is for a thing to be of a certain familiar kind, we have somewhat less the embarrassing and confused feeling that when we ask it we already know the answer. Nevertheless, the habits of thought which too often mislead us when we ask a purely conceptual question such as 'What is tolerance?' or 'What is honesty?' also, too often, mislead us when we ask, 'What is proper tolerance?' 'What is proper honesty?' Although we know the impossibility of a code which would make every decision in life, or even every decision in a certain sphere of life, as amenable to calculation as is a decision on the appropriate amount of fuel for moving a certain weight for a certain distance, the craving for such a code persists. And this is not surprising. Here in addition to the habit of thinking that the nature of every concept can be and should be set out in a set of principles another factor is at work. The more definite the instructions, the commandments, we have received from some authority, whether Moses, Christ or Hitler, the less the anxiety for our own responsibility. Consequently, if a teacher, aware of the danger of rules, speaks only or mainly in parables we may on this account be dissatisfied with him and clamour for philosopher, who shall provide us with principles which will enable us in every contingency of life to deduce with precision what we ought to do.

In this brief attempt to respond to the question 'What is it to ask what is tolerance?' and in general 'What is it to ask a "What-is . . . ?" question?' I may have given the impression that a 'What-is . . . ?' question is asked only by someone who wishes to review what is involved in a familiar concept. If so, I have given a false impression. For there is an important group of occasions when someone asks a 'What-is . . . ?' question because he is on the point of modifying an old concept, of developing a related but new concept. We may, for instance, imagine Cantor asking 'What is number?' when on the point of developing that concept of number in which infinite numbers in spite of their shocking eccentricities are still numbers. We may imagine Einstein asking himself 'What is simultaneity?' when on the point of developing that concept of simultaneity which permitted him to think of events as being simultaneous with respect to one observer and not with respect to another.

Often when we look back we regard with admiration those explorers who have ventured to leave old, well trodden paths of thought. But often when we meet them in the present we find difficulty in accepting what they offer us. Indeed we often find it difficult honestly to examine the gift horse which might have carried us off the roads we know to some point from which a still familiar landscape looks very different. Though our difficulty is sometimes, at least in part, an intellectual difficulty in grasping a profound modification in a fundamental concept of enormous scope, such as that of simultaneity, or number, or causal action, it is often in part not an intellectual difficulty. We often fear, resent, find intolerable, anyone's tampering with our old well-tried ideas.

These emotional factors which hinder our acceptance of changes, revolutions, in thought and practice are easily detected when the new idea presents very little intellectual difficulty. When Tod Sloan went from America to England and there rode racehorses he met with ridicule from those who had a long established conception of what it is to ride a horse properly. True, he soon modified that conception; for, crouched on his horses' shoulders 'like a monkey on a stick', he simply galloped down the opposition, and in a short time race-meetings all over the world demonstrated, as they still do, the influence of Tod Sloan. In this small revolution the sneers of the intolerant were speedily silenced by events. Larger revolutions may take longer and cost more.

In order to understand the shadowy, subtle world of our own selves we sometimes need to see as far from each other things which old habits of thought present as very close and to see things which old ideas have kept very separate as nevertheless remarkably close. When Christ said:

> Ye have heard that it was said by them of old time, Thou shalt not commit adultery. But I say unto you, that whosoever looketh on a woman to lust after her hath committed adultery with her already in his heart

he put into our minds a modified concept of adultery and, by implication, a modified concept of robbery, of violence, of intolerance, of forgiveness. He thereby, for better or for worse, increased our insight into ourselves and our demands upon ourselves. For before Christ spoke we could count ourselves far from adulterers and other sinners provided we had not *done* this or *done* that; but since he spoke we have felt we have no true picture of ourselves until we have looked within, searched our hearts.

For better or for worse, Freud carried the process still further. For before Freud spoke, most of us trusted the appearances in our own hearts, but after he spoke we were obliged to recognize how deceptive these too may be. At once the difficulties of reaching the things we would like to reach, amongst them real tolerance, became sadly clearer.

XIII

Mace, Moore, and Wittgenstein

I came to know Alec Mace at St Andrews in 1929 when I took up my first teaching post. Ever since I have felt a great respect for him as a thinker and a man.

A small article, 'Faculties and Instincts', which he published in *Mind* in 1931,[1] not only makes one think again about explanation by reference to faculties and instincts but throws a light upon all explanation. I would like to say something about that article here and also about a note on emotive and descriptive language which Mace contributed to an early number of *Analysis*. But I want still more to say something about Mace's essay 'On How We Know that Material Things Exist'[2] in *The Philosophy of G. E. Moore* and also something about a remark he made in a conversation many years ago at St. Andrews. Two or three of us had been discussing what we would then have described as the questions 'What do we mean when we call a thing "good"?' or 'What is the analysis of what we mean when we call a thing "good"?' The discussion had gone on for some time and had become rather warm when Mace remarked, with that shadow of a smile which those who know him will know, that it seemed to him that we need to put together not the true, the good, and the beautiful but the beautiful, the good, and the comic. We were not then able to talk much longer but Mace's comparison stayed in my mind and about twenty years later when I was giving the Gifford Lectures at Aberdeen I recommended the comparison of one who says of something 'It's good', with one who says of something 'It's amusing'. I did not make the point of the comparison clearly enough, for when the time for questions came no one said much about it. Perhaps

---

[1] 'Faculties and Instincts', *Mind*, 1931, XL, pp. 37–48.

[2] 'On How We Know that Material Things Exist', in Schilpp, P. A. (ed.), *The Philosophy of G. E. Moore*, Cambridge University Press, London, 1942.

everyone thought the comparison just another presentation of a subjective theory of value. The question 'Can one prove that something is funny?' sounds a bit like a joke, and it is only on second thoughts that one realizes that one who says of, for instance, a play, 'It's very funny', is not saying something so unchallengeable as 'I felt I'd die of laughing' nor so much at the mercy of the reactions of others as 'It will have them all rolling in the aisles'. And if a consideration of one who says of something 'It's comic' or 'It's tragic' throws light on one who says of something 'It's good', does it not also throw light on one who says of something 'It's sweet', 'It's bitter', 'It's yellow', 'It's hot', 'It's heavy', 'It's square'? We know how many philosophical difficulties can be expressed in the form 'Are questions of this kind objective or are they subjective?' One is inclined to think that the statement 'It's amusing' is as subjective as 'It's popular'. And one finds it is not.

However much a remark seems to light up in a flash a bit of country which though familiar to us has bewildered us, we may need to explore that bit of country step by step in daylight. There is not time to do that now with Mace's remark. But I do not want to leave it without saying something about another feature of it, namely, what it shows as to how one can meet philosophical difficulty.

Anyone who offers a rule for analysing questions of a certain sort and anyone who offers an analysis of a particular question such as 'Was it wrong to drop the bomb?' equates a question in one form with a question in another form and thus offers a comparison. Anyone who says that questions of one kind, for instance questions of praise and blame, are a species of questions of another kind, for instance questions as to matters of fact, classifies questions of the first kind and thus offers a comparison between them and other members of the class in which he puts them.

By analysis and classification, and by attempts at analysis and classification, we can go a long way in philosophy. But we can also reach a situation in which philosophical problems appear insoluble until we notice their affinity to, and then their difference from, riddles and see the value of a more primitive procedure in which we compare types of question, types of knowledge, to others without equating them to others or even classifying them with others.

Comparisons can be suggested without asserting anything, even without uttering a word. Imagine that as someone walks by us you laugh and that I say 'Why laugh?'. You may then, without a word, imitate the person who walked by, and this imitation, whether it is a close imitation or an extreme caricature, may show me what had escaped me. Even when a comparison is made in words nothing need be asserted. When William James called the riddle 'Does a man who walks round a tree on which there is a squirrel which keeps its face always towards him, walk round the squirrel?' a 'metaphysical' problem, he was not asserting that that problem is a metaphysical problem. Nor was he making the feeble assertion that the riddle is in some way like a metaphysical problem.

This remarking of affinities or of differences not readily marked in ordinary language has never been absent from philosophy. Indeed philosophy, whether of the kind which asks 'Does real honesty exist?' or 'Does real love exist?' or of the very different though still like kind which asks 'Does real knowledge exist?', springs from a dissatisfaction associated with normal classification and an ordinary use of words. Without those whose thought in this way sets a cat among the pigeons philosophy would not begin. Questions raised by comparison not on established lines can be met, and in extreme cases must be met, by comparison not on established lines.

The danger of thinking in comparisons which are not presented in statements which are to be taken literally is that such thinking may become too loose. But when in Mace there is evasion of statement, there is nonetheless immense determination to look and look again at what is under discussion until what has been obscure becomes clear. This is best known to those who have discussed matters with him, but some illustration of it may be found in his essay 'On How We Know that Material Things Exist' in *The Philosophy of G. E. Moore*.[1]

This essay, though focused on Moore, is about philosophical difficulty and how it may be met. It begins by drawing attention to a fact which though it had been familiar to all of us who had studied Moore had not sufficiently mystified us. It is this: Moore insisted that on many occasions we know things about,

---

[1] 'On How We Know that Material Things Exist', in Schilpp, P. A. (ed.), *The Philosophy of G. E. Moore*, Cambridge University Press, London, 1942.

for instance, the past, or the material world, and at the same time said that we, in a sense, do not know what it is we know on these occasions, and also do not know how we know what on these occasions we know. Mace quotes Moore's words 'We are all in this strange position that we do *know* many things, with regard to which we *know* further that we must have had evidence for them, and yet we do not know *how* we know them, i.e. we do not know what the evidence was.'

Mace agrees that there are several sorts of situation which one might be inclined to describe in this way. He reminds us that any plain man who is asked how he knows that the Great Pyramid existed before he was born 'may for a moment at least be at a loss for an answer', and that 'If we take a couple of glances at some material thing and then are asked how we know that this thing existed throughout the time between glances we are again at a loss for an immediate answer' and that when we are actually looking at things we may be nonplussed and perplexed when asked to say how we know that they exist at the times when we are actually perceiving them'.

At the same time Mace reminds us that we all do acquire much knowledge of material things, and of the past. He reminds us that whenever we are in doubt as to whether what is before us is part of a material thing, for instance a human hand, we know very well how to change this doubt into knowledge. In short, he reminds us that in a certain familiar, workaday sense we do know the evidence for the things we say about material things before us or behind us or in the past, and do know how we know these things, and do know what we know when we know these things.

In spite of Moore's questions as to how we know what we know when we know things about the past and what we mean when we talk about these things he would have gone thus far with Mace. See for instance Moore's *Some Main Problems of Philosophy*, p. 205. But Mace goes farther.

He reminds us (p. 285) that the plain man who is nonplussed by a question as to how he knows that the Great Pyramid existed before he was born 'would not be completely nonplussed', and that 'if he could not say precisely what the evidence was upon which he was relying he could say something regarding the sort of evidence that is relevant to the case'.

L

He agrees (p. 297) that the process by which we come to know even the simplest things about the material world (or the past) is complicated. He says, 'The details of the way in which these things are discovered admit of long and tedious description and for precise analysis require perhaps to be expressed in the elaborate notation of factorial analysis.' But he reminds us that the difficulties we may feel or find when we try to say how we know what we know not only do not prevent our achieving this knowledge but also do not prevent our having a good deal to say about how we achieve it.

Even this is still something which could be accepted as 'in a certain sense true of course' by someone who, like Moore, says that we do not know how we know what we know.

But Mace on his last page takes a further step. After saying that Moore's certainties are the certainties of the plain man and his doubts and hesitancies are the doubts and hesitancies of the plain man, he says:

> But what is more important than this is the fact that Moore's doubts would be resolved in the plain man's way.
>
> If Moore's methods are correct, the conclusion would seem to follow that the function of the philosopher is not to find new and technical evidence either for or against commonsense beliefs but to incite or provoke the plain man to find the answers to the questions posed—the answers which he 'naturally' gives if sufficiently pressed and kept to the point.

The significance of what Mace says here may easily be missed. For his words may convey the impression that the suggestion which he is making as to how philosophical difficulties may be met is a suggestion which can easily be inferred from a knowledge of Moore's methods. But the method here suggested, though like Moore's in that one who adopts it listens very carefully to what the plain man has to say, is also profoundly unlike the method we associate with Moore because he so long followed it. Moore to the last retained his willingness to think again about answers to philosophical questions and also about the way in which they may be met. But in his autobiography in *The Philosophy of G. E. Moore* (p. 33) he says, speaking of Wittgenstein,

He has made me think that what is required for the
solution of philosophical problems which baffle me, is a
method quite different from any that I have ever used—
a method which he himself uses successfully, but which I
have never been able to understand clearly enough to use
it myself.

Most of the problems which continued to trouble Moore
were either problems as to how we know things of a certain
kind, for instance things about the material world or the past,
or problems as to what we know when we know things of a
certain kind. And I believe that he was right in thinking that
these connected problems would not have baffled him as they
did but for a limitation in his idea as to how these problems
can be met.

When Moore felt baffled by a difficulty as to how we know
propositions of a certain kind, for instance propositions about
the past, what was the line of thought which had led him into
this unfortunate condition? In the first place he had considered
very carefully whether propositions of the kind in question
are analysable into, deducible from, or disguised forms of,
propositions of a kind which raise no difficulty, or at least do
not raise the same difficulty; and he had found himself unable
to accept any suggestion of this sort. For instance, he very much
doubted whether propositions about material things are analysable into propositions about sensations and whether propositions about the past are disguised propositions about the present.

In the second place he had also, before acknowledging
himself baffled, considered the suggestion that our knowledge
of propositions of the kind in question is indirect, that it is
reached by induction. And this suggestion, too, he had been
unable to accept.

In the third place Moore had considered and rejected the
suggestion that we do not have knowledge of propositions of the
kind in question. He had considered samples of propositions
of the kind in question and his certainty that we do have a
knowledge of propositions of that kind had remained quite
unshaken. These results may be summed up by saying of propositions of the kind in question, e.g. propositions about material
things or propositions about the past or propositions about good

and evil, that they are not analysable into or classifiable as propositions which do not provoke the same difficulty, that they are not derivable by deduction nor yet by induction from such propositions, and that nevertheless they are known—that they are what they are and are known in their own way.

Moore was again and again driven toward this sort of answer. But it did not satisfy him. It was not that he thought it untrue. It was not merely that he was not quite certain of its truth, because he was not quite certain that propositions of the kind in question are not analysable into, and not derivable by induction from, propositions which do not raise the same difficulty. It was that this sort of answer left him still feeling that he did not know as he wanted to know how propositions of the kind in question are known. He felt the answer inadequate and he also did not see how to add to it so as to remove that inadequacy.

In this double respect he was like those philosophers who have avoided this sort of answer by adopting one of those answers which Moore rejected. Much as they differed from each other and from Moore, they all, like Moore, felt that the sort of answer Moore was driven to accept is inadequate, and they also could not see any way to add to it so as to remove that inadequacy. This group includes a great many philosophers who have attempted to deal with problems as to how we know what we claim to know in this sphere or in that. But not all—not all in the same degree. G. F. Stout, for instance, was rather different. Wittgenstein was very different. True one might read Stout and then think to oneself, 'All he does is to say that propositions about material things are not reducible to, deducible from, propositions about sense experience, and that they are not known indirectly, inductively, from propositions about sense experience, and that they are known somehow "immediately" and yet "in and through" sense experience.' He makes no attempt to enlighten us on what it is to know "immediately" and yet "in and through" sense experience.' But Stout does make an attempt to do this. Indeed, someone might complain: 'Stout becomes so engaged in describing how we reach our beliefs about material things, about other people, about the past, that his work reads more like a piece of psychology than an attempt to show that or how these beliefs are *justified.*'

Wittgenstein's work is very different. And yet there is a remarkable similarity. This similarity comes out if one thinks of someone who having read Wittgenstein says: 'This man, when he is asked a philosophical question as to how from the data we have we know what we claim to know about the past or the material world, shows wonderfully well how misleading is the answer "Indirectly" or "As from reflections in a mirror we know what is behind us on the road". So much so that one would have expected him to give a positivistic answer to the philosophical question and to say that propositions about things of the kind in question are analysable into, reducible to, and thus deducible from, propositions about the data from which they are derived. But in fact he does not. He was on one occasion asked "Are propositions about material things entailed by propositions about our sensations?" and his reply was not "Yes". It was "We know them from our sensations" or "through our sensations". I cannot exactly remember his words but they were very like that. He seemed to think that in order to solve a philosophical problem or philosophical difficulty as to how we reach knowledge in a certain sphere it is enough to show the incorrectness of solutions which have been offered and then say "But is not this what we here *call* knowledge?" For instance, what more than this does he do when in his *Philosophical Investigations* (p. 137) he asks "What is *called* a justification here?"'

This is, of course, a caricature, a mischievous caricature, of Wittgenstein's procedure. Wittgenstein did what this caricaturist says he did. But he did much more. He fought the habit of thinking on the following pattern: 'The statements we make about material things cannot be justified deductively from the sort of data on which they are based. So they must be hypotheses justified inductively from that sort of data. Or else they are not justified at all and are at best expressions of beliefs which are often useful guides to life.' And in this battle he often put a challenging question of the form: 'If this isn't justification of this sort of statement what would be justification of this sort of statement?' But when he asked such a question he did so against a background of work in which he had shown us in instance after instance how easily we come to have, temporarily at least, a cramped grasp of the varieties within the unity of a kind—a kind of thing or kind of activity, for instance the playing of a game, the defending of a position, the justification of an assertion, the discovery of a truth, the attainment of knowledge. Moore in describing Wittgenstein's work in *Philosophical Papers* (p. 256) writes,

> I cannot possibly do justice to the extreme richness of illustration and comparison he used; he was really succeeding in giving what he called a 'synoptic' view of things which we all know.

The phrase 'a synoptic view of things which we all know' reminds one of words Moore used early in his philosophical career when he wished to explain the purpose of asking what an expression means even when one is quite familiar with its meaning. In *Some Main Problems of Philosophy* he writes (p. 205), '.... obviously with a notion itself, it may be quite readily conveyed to us by a word, even though we cannot analyse it or say exactly how it is related to or distinguished from other notions'. Had Moore here written not 'say exactly' but 'see exactly' and had he here recognized another way besides analysis to a synoptic view of where a notion stands among other notions, his way of working on difficulties as to how we reach knowledge of this kind and knowledge of that kind might not have suffered from that limitation which so much affected his work and the work of others.

It is easy to exaggerate here. Moore himself exaggerates the difference between himself and Wittgenstein when he says that Wittgenstein used a method quite different from any that he, Moore, had ever used. In the first place, as we have noticed already, the examination of any proposed analysis or classification of a notion or a class of propositions involves comparisons. For instance one cannot examine the 'theory' or 'theorem' that any assertion that a thing is good is equivalent to an assertion that it is approved by most people without comparing these two sorts of assertion. And whether or no the proposed analysis or classification turns out to be correct the comparison may be, and often is, enlightening. In the second place it is not true that when Moore had come to the conclusion that a class of propositions is 'unanalysable' he then never had anything more to say. When Moore wrote his essay 'The Conception of Intrinsic Value' he was still opposing any analysis of predicates of value into naturalistic predicates, but in his essay he is comparing predicates of value with other sorts of predicate. The essay is, I submit, an extremely valuable comparative study of the difference or differences between predicates of value and other predicates. Nevertheless Moore's feeling that he succeeds only if he can 'say' or 'say exactly' or 'define' what the difference is has two mischievous effects. It makes him disparage his own achievement. He says that he can see that there is a difference but that he 'cannot see *what* it is' (p. 274). I suggest that what troubles him is not so much that he cannot *see* as that he cannot *say* what the difference is, I mean cannot say what the difference is in that way which people are regarding as the proper way of making a thing clear when they say that they 'cannot define', 'cannot state precisely', 'cannot say exactly' what they had in mind when they made a certain remark, for instance 'Hemingway's work is sentimental' or 'Jack has *changed* since he married that woman'. Two things are worth noticing about the occasions when people say this sort of thing. First, sometimes when someone says, and says truly, that he cannot 'define' or 'state precisely' or 'find the right word for' what he has in mind, he has nevertheless already made perfectly clear what he has in mind. Certainly he sometimes has not, but to remember this only reminds us more clearly that sometimes he has, that sometimes there is absolutely no need for him to say any more. Secondly, sometimes, often, when someone says and says truly that he 'cannot define', 'cannot state precisely', 'cannot say properly' what he has in mind he then abandons any attempt to do what he still might do to make clearer, to make quite clear, what he has in mind. Feeling that he has failed, or that words have failed him, he stops trying to illustrate what he has in mind or to make it clear by reference to parallel cases. Moore seldom permits himself to say anything so inconclusive, so near to saying nothing, as 'How like is one who tells us that a play is good to one who tells us that it is funny!' And Moore seldom permits himself to say anything as extravagant as what James permitted himself to say when he called the riddle about the squirrel a 'metaphysical' problem or so extravagant as that which Wittgenstein permitted himself to say when he called principles of logic 'rules of grammar', or as that which a person permits himself to say when he says that statements about chairs and tables are statements about our sensations or that statements about good and evil are statements about our feelings. Moore upon the whole confined himself to opposing or at least questioning such extravagant assertions. And this opposition was of very great value. For such assertions may on the one hand mislead and on the other hand go unappreciated, unless they are opposed by a person of common sense, whether he be one who has never taken a hand in philosophy before or an old hand like Moore. But such a person need not confine himself to such opposition. He need not confine himself to saying, nor confine himself to showing, that statements as to what is good and bad are not merely statements about our feelings. He may hesitate when asked to go on but, as Mace reminds us, he can go on. For instance, suppose that someone who has never read any philosophy is asked, 'How does one know what lies behind one in the past?' He may reply, 'By memory.' And if he is then asked, 'And how does one know that one's memory portrays faithfully what is behind one in the past?' he might then reply, 'Well I suppose one comes to know that one's memory can be trusted as to what is behind one in the past much as one comes to know that one's driving-mirror can be trusted as to what is behind one on a road.' This answer reminds one of a philosopher who says that our knowledge of the past is indirect. Indeed, as one might have expected, the answers which non-philosophers give when pressed to answer philosophical questions again and again remind one of the answers which philosophers have given. So much so that one may wonder why Mace has such high hopes of help from 'the plain man', such a respect for a 'common-sense' method of meeting philosophical difficulties. What is the way of meeting philosophical difficulties which Mace has in mind when he speaks of 'a plain man's way'?

The way in question is not one which a non-philosopher is certain to adopt nor one which a philosopher is certain not to adopt. It is a way which a philosophical training may discourage one from adopting and which the absence of philosophical training may leave one free to adopt. But what is this way like?

Suppose that someone is urged to say something indicating

the differences between (a) the way one answers a question as to what is so in the material world and (b) the way one answers a question as to appearances in one's own mind and (c) the way one answers a question as to appearances in the minds of others. He may reply somewhat as follows: 'Well to begin with if you are asked "Is there a difference between the taste of this and the taste of that?" you cannot answer this question in the simple way you can answer the question "Do you taste a difference between this and that?" or "Does it appear to you that there is a difference between the taste of this and that?".' And he may go on to say that one of the differences here is that although in order to answer the question 'Is there a difference of taste between this and that?' one may and should, if one has not already done so, taste both this and that as one should when asked 'Do you taste a difference between this and that', one must, in the case of the question as to whether there is a difference as opposed to the question whether one tastes a difference pay some regard to what other people and animals have to say in the matter, though not that regard one must pay in order to answer a question as to whether Jack or Jill or most people taste a difference between this and that.

These remarks sound childish—I mean they sound like the sort of thing one might say to a very young child when explaining to him the difference between lions in dreams and lions in the jungle or between imaginary voices and real voices. They tell us, who are not children, only what we very well know already. And yet they are to the purpose. They mention what is very relevant to what philosophers have had in mind when they have said that one cannot know or cannot know directly the material world, while one cannot but know what is in one's own mind at the moment.

But though these remarks are to the purpose are they adequate to the purpose? May they not meet with the response: 'This is all very well but go on. What is the difference between the way in which one must, as you put it, "pay regard to what others have to say" when answering the question "Is there a difference between the taste of this and that?" and the way one must pay regard to what others have to say when answering the question "Does Jack, does Jill, do most people taste a difference between this and that?"'

Certainly these remarks may meet with this response. They may not. They may meet instead with the response 'Ah that's it. That points to those differences and affinities between knowledge of one's own mind, knowledge of the material world, and knowledge of the minds of others which some philosophers have naturally but misleadingly indicated by saying that knowledge of one's own mind is direct while knowledge of the material world is indirect and knowledge of the minds of others doubly indirect.' But though these remarks *may* meet with such a welcome it must be confessed that they are likely to meet with a complaint or at least a request to go on.

However, there is nothing to stop us from going on. There is nothing to discourage us from going on with further remarks of the same sort unless we think that however much we go on with remarks of this sort they will never meet the need expressed by the questions 'How do we know about material things? What is the difference between our knowledge of material things and other kinds of knowledge?'

Unfortunately we sometimes do come near to thinking this. The tendency to think on these lines does not show itself only in philosophy. It shows itself on many occasions when someone endeavours to meet a question as to what it is for things to differ in a certain way or what it is for a thing to be of a certain kind. Suppose that someone who very well knows what poetry is asks 'What is poetry?' or 'What is the difference between poetry and prose?' and that we reply 'Well if one were to write

> Whatever is to come, is not;
> How can it then be mine?
> The present moment's all my lot,
> And that, as fast as it is got,
> Phyllis, is wholly thine.

one would be writing poetry, while if one were to write "The future, since it does not now exist, is not now at my disposal. Only the present moment is. But that, Phyllis, is always at once wholly yours" then one would be writing prose.' We should not be thought to have said anything untrue nor anything altogether beside the point. But our answer would be likely to be called 'hardly an answer' and 'inadequate'. And certainly it does little to bring before the mind the range of poetry and the range of prose. We might, of course, add many other examples of poetry and of prose. We might without attempting a definition of poetry add remarks about the examples. We might draw attention to the presence or absence of rhyme or of rhythm of a certain sort. Many might then find our answer more satisfactory, more adequate. And yet there might be in many still the thought that any answer of this sort must at best be a second best.

And this is very natural. One may of course teach by examples the meaning of the word 'poetry' to one who does not know what is poetry and what is not, as one may by examples teach a child the meaning of 'bow wow' or 'moo cow'. But if someone already knows what is poetry and what isn't when he asks 'What is poetry?' then surely what he needs cannot be provided by pointing to examples of what is and is not poetry? If someone who already knows which arguments are syllogistic and which are not now asks 'What is syllogistic argument?', shall we help him much if we set before him from his own repertoire examples of argument which is syllogistic and argument which is not? Without saying that such examples would be useless to him it is surely very likely that an answer which provides a definition of the term 'syllogistic argument' will meet his need more quickly and more adequately. How admirably does the definition of 'cousin' provided by the *Oxford Dictionary* enable us to review the varieties of cousin. Examples, on the other hand, even when numerous and well chosen, always put a tax on our power to extract the relevant from the irrelevant, to abstract the universal from the particular. One who gives a definition of the difference between things of a certain kind and things not of that kind specifies, states, just what is, and, by implication, what is not necessary to that difference in a way in which no one who does not give a definition does.

So it is not surprising that often when someone who has been asked a question as to the nature of a certain difference, for instance, the difference between poetry and prose, feels that he cannot define that difference he is somewhat apologetic in his reply. He may say, 'I am afraid I cannot define the difference'; and even if he then goes on to try to give some account of that difference he often does so with an air of providing what is inevitably only a second best. Indeed he may be so discouraged by his inability to define the difference that he abandons any attempt to give an account of it and says, 'Well there is a difference but I'm afraid I cannot explain what it is.' He may even say that he does not know what it is or even that no one knows what it is. A certain critic—it was Humbert Wolfe—when reviewing the poems of Laura Riding, found himself obliged to reject as incorrect several definitions of poetry. He then came very near to drawing the conclusion that we do not know what poetry is. A philosopher who has rejected as either incorrect or futile every definition of the difference between necessary and contingent statements may be tempted to suggest that we have no reason to think that there is a difference and even that there is no difference. Even such extreme reactions to an inability to meet by a definition the need of one who asks the nature of a difference are understandable.

It has however often been remarked, for instance by judges, that the fact that we cannot define a difference does not mean that we do not know what that difference is. Whether or no we have defined or can define the difference between an elephant and a kangaroo or a mammoth there is a difference and we know that difference. Is it true perhaps that we inevitably have a *better* grasp of a difference, of a notion, we have defined than we have of one we have not? But this too is not so. When we have defined the difference between squares and rectangles by saying that squares are rectangles which have all their sides equal, we do not have a better grasp of that difference than we have of the difference between sides which are equal and sides which are not, whether or no we have defined the differences between sides which are equal and sides which are not. Is it true that when someone already knows the difference between things of a certain kind and things not of that kind, in the sense that he can always say whether a thing is of that kind or not, then no review of examples can improve his grasp of that difference as a definition could? But this, too, is not so. A person who can recognize arguments which are syllogistic and arguments which are not *may* by a careful consideration of different examples of each come to see better the relations between arguments of the two sorts just as much as one who finds or is offered a definition of syllogistic argument.

Indeed it may happen that the improvement in our grasp of the varieties of a kind produced by the consideration of examples is greater than the improvement produced by a definition. For it may happen that the definition provides only a way of saying what has already been seen while the examples show what has not been seen. It may happen that someone notices a difference—perhaps a difference between ways to knowledge or ways of life—for which there is at present no name and *a fortiori* no definition. In such a situation the idea that nothing but a definition will enable one to see clearly what one wishes to see may discourage one from looking again and thinking afresh in that way in which, at such a juncture, one so much needs to look again and think afresh.

Wittgenstein and his followers were anxious to make clear the mischief this idea may make and, in particular, the mischief it may make in philosophy, which is an inquiry in which one is again and again concerned to study some disturbing difference or affinity which language as it stands does not mark and even obscures.

Logicians provided us with an excellent system of words and symbols for describing the differences and affinities between the various forms of demonstrative and non-demonstrative, deductive and inductive, justification for beliefs. But all this good work did not clear up the difficulties philosophers felt when they asked themselves questions as to the *ultimate* justification for our beliefs—our beliefs about the past, our beliefs about the minds of others. It left them still hesitant as to whether this ultimate justification is deductive or inductive and it did nothing to diminish an inclination to think that unless the process by which we reach our beliefs is deductive or at least inductive then it is not a process of justification it all.

Some philosophers like Moore freed themselves from this confining idea as to what a process leading to belief must be like if it is to give knowledge. But even one who has freed himself from this idea may still have the confining idea that the knowledge desired by one who asks a question as to what it is for a thing to be of a certain kind or as to how a thing is done can be provided only by a definition, an analysis. And such a person is likely to feel that though on many occasions we know things about the past, the minds of others, material things, nevertheless, unless we can (a) define, analyse, what we know on these occasions and (b) define, analyse, what it is to know what we know on these occasions, then we (a) do not know what we know on these occasions and (b) do not know how we know it. Moore was often very nearly in this position, though in his later years, influenced by Wittgenstein, he was moving out of it.

Unfortunately Wittgenstein and his followers were so anxious to draw attention to the mischievous effects of the idea that a better grasp of what it is for a thing to be of a certain kind can be gained only by finding a correct definition of what it is for a thing to be of that kind that they sometimes gave the impression that whenever no such definition exists it is a waste of time to look for one. But incorrect definitions can be extremely valuable to us provided we come to see how they are incorrect, and this we can do even when we cannot define that incorrectness. We betray a still limited idea about how we can gain a better grasp of what it is for a thing to be of a certain kind if we represent as inevitably useless all attempts to define the indefinable.

Mace does not do this. He does indeed make it clear that he does not believe that when we are faced with a philosophical question 'Do we on these occasions have real knowledge and if so what is it that we know and how do we know it?' then we can achieve the desired synoptic view of what we know and how we know it only if we can find definitions of what we know and how we know it which are both illuminating and perfectly correct. But he does not induce in us a fear that any search for such definitions is bound to hinder our efforts to meet the need which prompts such questions by saying what 'naturally occurs' to us, when such questions are asked. What naturally occurs to us when we are asked 'What is knowledge?' or 'What is knowledge of this kind?' is of the same variety as what occurs to us if we are asked 'What is deductive reasoning?' or 'What is poetry?' or 'What is drama?' or 'What is life?' When we are asked such questions we offer definitions, mention characteristic features, employ similes and metaphors, present parables and examples.

If we follow this natural course we shall soon hear voices telling us that this or that part of our procedure is inappropriate, useless. For instance we shall be told that if we wish to gain a more than piecemeal, a synoptic view of life, then we should abandon the reading of novels and plays which merely represent happenings in life as familiar as a young officer's falling in love with a beautiful married woman, and turn to more philosophical works. (Here we may remember that Tolstoy was vexed because people gave more attention to his stories than to his philosophical writings.) But if we take this advice we shall soon hear someone telling us that we are following a wrong and even ludicrous course since a philosophical treatment of questions such as 'What is life?' or 'What is the meaning of life?' is bound to end in answers which are unverifiable and meaningless or in answers which when they are not incorrect are trite. We may indeed be told that such questions as 'What is life?' or 'What is the meaning of life?' are still asked only because people have the idea that these questions have an answer when in fact they have no answer. We may be given the impression that when such questions are asked there is nothing to be done beyond bringing to light the confusions which prompt people to ask them.

Here we may remember that some people have gathered from Wittgenstein the impression that one should not expect from philosophy anything more than (1) the cure of certain persistent illusions as to the nature of philosophical statements and questions and (2) the cure of certain intermittent illusions as to the nature of non-philosophical statements and questions —illusions which overcome us in idle moments. Some people get the mistaken impression that one cannot expect from psychoanalysis anything more than the restoration of a normal view of life. Some people get the mistaken impression that one cannot expect from philosophy anything more than the restoration of a normal view of knowledge. Mace does not give this impression. He reminds us that in philosophy we are concerned only with what is as familiar to us as the way in which we settle doubts as to whether what appears to be a dagger is a real dagger or a reflection in a mirror or a figment of the mind. So he discourages the idea that in philosophy we make discoveries, gain knowledge, like one who with X-ray photographs learns more of the nature of matter. But on the other hand he does not give the impression that in philosophy the best we can hope for is the restoration of a normal view of the various species of knowledge. On the contrary he gives the impression that if when we encounter a philosophical question, whether it be as sober-sounding as 'How do we know the material world?' or as crazy-sounding as 'Do we know the material world?', then if we succeed in meeting it we shall obtain a better view of the familiar processes with which it is concerned than any view of them we had in our normal, common-sensical, pre-philosophical days. And he encourages us to believe that we can succeed if we permit ourselves to use all the resources available to us.

Mace is one of those who, whether they are doing philosophy or not doing philosophy, combat our inclination to allow habits of thought and talk to confine our efforts to see better than we have before what things are like.